HOW GOD
TEACHES
US
TO PRAY

A Month of Devotions on Praying with God's Power and Guidance

HOW GOD TEACHES US TO PRAY

Lessons from the Lives of Francis and Edith Schaeffer

Founders of L'Abri Fellowship

by

L. G. Parkhurst, Jr.

Designed as a Classic Textbook on How to Pray Effectively

WORD PUBLISHING
Nelson Word Ltd
Milton Keynes, England
WORD AUSTRALIA
Kilsyth, Australia
WORD COMMUNICATIONS LTD
Vancouver, B.C., Canada
STRUIK CHRISTIAN BOOKS (PTY) LTD
Cape Town, South Africa
JOINT DISTRIBUTORS SINGAPORE –
ALBY COMMERCIAL ENTERPRISES PTE LTD
and
CAMPUS CRUSADE, ASIA LTD
CHRISTIAN MARKETING NEW ZEALAND LTD
Havelock North, New Zealand
JENSCO LTD
Hong Kong
SALVATION BOOK CENTRE
Malaysia

HOW GOD TEACHES US TO PRAY

Copyright © L.G. Parkhurst Jr., 1993.

Published by Nelson Word Ltd., Milton Keynes, England, 1993.

ISBN 0-85009-585-9   (Australia ISBN 1-86258-265-3)

Unless otherwise indicated, Scripture quotations are from the Holy Bible: New International Version, copyright © 1973, 1978, 1984 by International Bible Society and used by permission.

Other Scripture quotations are from the New American Standard Bible (NASB), © The Lockman Foundation 1960, 1962, 1963, 1968, 1971, 1972, 1973, 1975, 1977.

Reproduced, printed and bound in Great Britain for Nelson Word Ltd. by Cox and Wyman Ltd., Reading.

93 94 95 96 / 10 9 8 7 6 5 4 3 2 1

CONTENTS

EDITH SCHAEFFER'S THOUGHTS ON PRAYER

So many times I have been reminded that we do not give anything up for the Lord, not really, because He repays us a hundredfold in *this* life; in the life to come, we cannot even imagine the surprises He has in store for us.[1]

Financial needs, spiritual needs, changed lives, wandering ones brought back, work unfolded and Workers blended together—all directly in answer to prayer alone. With Hudson Taylor we can say by experience that God *is able* to move man by prayer alone. What a glorious and all-powerful God we have—and One who makes and *keeps* promises. Let us study His promises more and search our hearts to see if we harbour any doubt in the place of trust.[2]

But, looking back, the wonder of it is the realisation that God was answering prayer for direction, not with big supernatural signs, but quiet and definite leading . . . We have a Person to whom we may communicate, and our cries and requests do make a difference in history.[3]

PREFACE

In 1955, Francis and Edith Schaeffer founded L'Abri Fellowship in Switzerland to demonstrate the reality of God through prayer. God so blessed their work that they began writing their many books in the 1960s. Because of the wide circulation of Dr Francis Schaeffer's books in several foreign languages, many people associate their work only with logical arguments for God's existence, with honest answers to honest questions, and with good reasons to be a Christian. However, time and again Dr Schaeffer said that his books did not stand alone: they stood with those of his wife.

Edith Schaeffer's books show the existence of God through answers to prayer and transformed lives. She wrote about the founding of L'Abri and told how they based their work on prayer. They *prayed* for God to send the people of His choice to them; they *prayed* for God to send the money they needed without soliciting for funds; they *prayed* for God to give them His direct leading and plan; and they *prayed* for God to send the co-workers of His choice.[1] Through daily prayer and God's provision in answer to prayer, they intended to manifest the presence of God to those around them, especially to unbelievers.

With their combined methods of arguing for God's existence and then living every day on the basis of God really being there in daily communication, they strove to maintain a careful balance between the intellectual and the devotional life.[2] When we study their books and lives together, we find good and sufficient reasons to bow before Jesus Christ as our Lord and Saviour. By the grace of God, their total work demonstrates substantially the transforming power of the Word of Truth and the Holy Spirit in leading sinners to the Saviour and establishing Christians in faith and obedience.

Time magazine labelled Francis Schaeffer 'the missionary to intellectuals'. Because of this stature, his philosophy and theology have often been analysed or criticised in academic books and journal articles. However, no book has looked closely at the Schaeffers' prayer principles in the light of their answers to prayer.[3] In some of her books, Edith Schaeffer illustrated their concern to be people of prayer in the normal course of daily living, but their answers to prayer and combined teachings on prayer are scattered in the midst of their discussions on other topics, in both their books and their tapes. *How God Teaches Us to Pray* takes thirty-one examples of different types of answered prayer from their lives and works, and shows how God teaches us to pray. Rather than just analyse or criticise their prayer principles, I hope to inspire you to pray daily with greater fervency. I have written with sincere appreciation for their life of prayer, and have not tried to write a critical biography. I have, however, shown many of the difficulties they faced as they prayed for a greater reality of God in their lives.

Francis Schaeffer never wrote a book on prayer, but he did preach on prayer.[4] When we read the letters of Francis Schaeffer beginning in the 1950s, we see the great importance he placed on prayer and reading devotional books (especially in the young Christian's life), for spiritual growth and renewal.[5] From Edith Schaeffer's letters home from Europe and later from her L'Abri Family Letters, from her books *L'Abri* and *The Tapestry*, from her books on various subjects, and through her and Fran's personal ministry, we have a record of many answers to their prayers and a wealth of information from which to select some of the best examples and applications for this devotional book on prayer.[6] I encourage you to read about their many other answers to prayers in their books.

Hudson Taylor with his China Inland Mission, George Müller with his orphanages, Charles Finney with his revivals, C. H. Spurgeon with his sermons, and Andrew Murray with his devotional books have inspired those of their own and succeeding generations to pray fervently for God to meet the needs of others. Likewise, the Schaeffers inspire our generation and will inspire succeeding generations to be ministers of intercession.[7] A. W. Tozer wrote:

> Next to the Holy Scriptures the greatest aid to the life of faith may be Christian biography. It is indeed notable that a large part of the Bible itself is given over to the life and labours of prophets, patriarchs and kings—who they were, what they did and said, how they prayed and toiled and suffered and triumphed at last![8]

How God Teaches Us to Pray demonstrates that the Schaeffers' lives may be their most important argument for God's existence.[9] Through God's marvellous and gracious intervention in their lives, we see clearly that God exists, and we discover some principles upon which He acts in people's lives.

As we contemplate how God prepared the Schaeffers for a ministry of prayer, we must marvel at two things God placed on Edith's heart that made their work spread beyond Switzerland and still speak to us today. First, God inspired her to write carefully detailed letters home to her mother

14

and family in America. These letters described God's work in their lives, their work, some ways God answered prayers, and some ways God bestowed grace in their afflictions and overcame Satan's attacks. Second, Edith wrote these letters in ways that would enable her mother to see things through her eyes and experience her emotions. She filled her letters with life and vitality, and carried this God-given talent and technique into her books. By inspiring her to write these long letters in the way she did, God taught her to write books in a way that would interest and involve thousands of readers for many years. God's guiding Edith to write to her mother preserved for us a record of answers to prayer that glorify God.[10] Even though *How God Teaches Us to Pray* is a devotional book with more than thirty-one brief answers to their prayers, I suggest you read *L'Abri* to see how these fit into the context of many other events in their lives and ministry. Her book *The Tapestry* is currently out of print in America.

Dr Schaeffer believed that a changed life was one of the most important arguments for God's existence, and he prayed that he would be able to show others both the love of God and the truth of God at the same time in the power of the Holy Spirit.[11] Because I have known the Schaeffers since 1978, and saw how they handled Dr Schaeffer's terminal cancer for more than five years; because I personally know how Edith has continued their ministry for many years since his death, I can testify that they have been and are consistent, honest witnesses to the transforming truth, power, and love of God in the best, worst, and most difficult of times.[12]

I have written *How God Teaches Us to Pray* to glorify God, and show how any believer can pray, live, and have as close a walk with God as the Schaeffers. They were called to a specific type of ministry, but each of us can know God as deeply, as personally, and as powerfully as they did. I hope that as you read the daily devotions in this book that you will praise the God who called them, empowered them, and inspired them to pray as they did so He could answer their prayers. I hope the Holy Spirit will move you to be a more dedicated person of prayer and student of the Word, and I pray you will always know God and His presence as intimately as the Schaeffers.

These devotions do not give little daily formulas for placing God under some kind of an obligation to bless you because you have prayed in a certain way. Teaching about prayer in the context of the Schaeffers' answers to prayer should remind all of us that God is not mechanical, but personal.

The answers to prayer in this book magnify God, because they were given to specific people absolutely devoted to glorifying God at every moment and witnessing for Christ at every opportunity in the power of the Holy Spirit (even though they were the first to say that they never did this perfectly—this remained their intention). I have never heard Francis or Edith Schaeffer pray a selfish prayer, and you will never find a selfish prayer request in their books or letters. If you will make a similar wholehearted commitment to God before beginning this book, if you will resolve to love, serve and glorify God unreservedly and unselfishly before you read the first chapter, then by the grace of Christ and through the indwelling Holy Spirit, you will gain far more than I could ever hope or imagine.

Since the Bible must be our primary authority for what constitutes acceptable prayer to God, in each chapter I have compared what they taught and experienced with the Bible's clear teachings about prayer. My goal in this devotional book is to encourage you, as a person of prayer, to pray daily and fervently according to the Scriptures and on the basis of God's steadfast love and faithfulness (which He demonstrated in the lives and teachings of the Schaeffers and L'Abri).

I have included three appendices to help you in the study of this book. Appendix I lists *some* principles of prayer and where to find them in the various chapters. I encourage you to look for more and write them in the margins of the appendix in their proper place. This appendix acts as a brief summary of each chapter regarding how to pray. Appendix II is a ten-week group study guide on prayer based on this book. It can be used individually and personally to help you apply the teachings in each chapter. If people who are practising prayer as they study discuss the ideas in each chapter as a group, then God will teach them many new things beyond the scope of this book as they talk to one another. If the book is to be used by a prayer group, then I would suggest you study only one chapter at each meeting to give you the most time for actually praying. Appendix III is a list of L'Abri branches and where to write each one; also included is the address of The Francis A. Schaeffer Foundation. Endnotes and an index to the Scriptures follow the appendices at the end of the book.

I do wish to acknowledge the help of two of Edith Schaeffer's former secretaries, who listened to and read portions of this book: my wife, Pat Parkhurst, and Ann Wells. My son and daughter, Jonathan and Kathryn, also made helpful comments as we read the manuscript together as a family. Any errors that remain are my own.

May this daily devotional book encourage you to pray as ardently as the Schaeffers and expect that God will answer and guide you as faithfully as He did them. May the Lord bless this book, as I seek to glorify Him by pointing out His work in their lives and what He can do in our lives through fervent prayer. I have included my own prayers at the close of each devotional as an expression of my thankfulness to God for teaching us how to pray.

With Love in the Risen Lamb,
L. G. Parkhurst, Jr.
Edmond, Oklahoma
1993

— 1 —

IF THE ANSWER IS NO

> Three times I pleaded with the Lord to take it
> away from me. But he said to me, 'My grace is
> sufficient for you, for my power is made perfect in
> weakness.' Therefore I will boast all the more
> gladly about my weaknesses, so that Christ's
> power may rest on me. That is why, for Christ's
> sake, I delight in weaknesses, in insults, in
> hardships, in persecutions, in difficulties. For
> when I am weak, then I am strong.
>
> 2 Corinthians 12:8–10

*I*n 1948, on the last Sunday Francis Schaeffer preached as the pastor of the old Bible Presbyterian Church in St Louis, Edith Schaeffer prayed and wept over his decision to leave the pastorate and become a mission administrator overseas. She fervently prayed for the Lord to intervene and keep them in America, because she believed Fran's gifts were for serving a church and preaching the Bible. As she reasoned with God, she pointed out that Fran loved people and really helped them, so why would He want Fran to be an administrator?

The Lord did not intervene and keep them in their church or find them a new church in America. *Literally*, God's answer to her prayer was a definite 'No'. They first went to Holland and then to Switzerland with the Independent Board for Presbyterian Foreign Missions. And by starting Children For Christ classes in churches all across war-torn Europe, they achieved one of their major goals. (This was a successful programme they had created in America which they were expanding, teaching and translating for European evangelical churches and homes.) But if God had answered her prayer *literally*, the work of L'Abri would not have begun in 1955, and Dr Schaeffer would not have developed his influential ideas through his study and discussions with people from all over the world.

God looked at the intention of Edith's heart and did not answer her prayer *to the letter*, but according to her spirit. In her pleading, Edith revealed her strong desire for God to show her husband how and where to serve Him in the best possible ways. The spirit of her prayer indicated that she did not want Fran's good influence diminished, but increased. Were her motives pure? Were they unmixed and unaffected by her desire not to be uprooted from home, friends and family? Perhaps not. But primarily, she wanted Fran empowered to serve Jesus Christ and meet people's needs in God's place for them, and she firmly believed America was God's place. She wanted God to put her husband where people would benefit from his compassionate care and solid Biblical teaching, and she knew how badly this was needed right where they were.

As for herself, she did pray that God would help her be submissive to the will of God and to her husband. Although God did not give her *exactly* what she prayed for by keeping them in America, He did fulfil the intention of her heart or the spirit of her prayer by empowering Fran to help people in Europe, and later by enabling him to help Americans in Europe and America. If God had granted her request to the letter, they would not have had the opportunity to receive something far greater and bless greater numbers.

God accomplished in the Schaeffers' lives exactly what He has promised every Christian, that He is able and willing to do 'immeasurably more than all we ask or imagine, according to his power that is at work within us' (Ephesians 3:20). Knowing this, Paul could even boast in his weaknesses. Can we believe this when we pray? Can we believe that God will grant us the good intentions of our hearts and answer our benevolent requests?

By His grace, God gave the Schaeffers power to accomplish much more for Him in a nontraditional way than if they had stayed in their church in St Louis. Even before they founded L'Abri, God used Fran's firm but tender ways as a pastor to meet the needs of hurting and searching young people from all over the world.

Sometimes God says 'No' because our hearts are not right with Him. We are asking selfishly, or our requests are wrong. We need to take time for self-examination in the light of His Word. But when we believe that our hearts or intentions are right and according to His will, we must believe that when God says 'No' to a specific request, He is only saying 'No' to our *literal* request and not to the right spirit of our prayers. Along with us, God wants to promote the best interests of all concerned. In praying for guidance, God eventually taught Edith, 'We feel that when one is praying for this sort of guidance, then "no" must be taken as from the Lord just as rapidly as "yes" and we must trust Him and thank Him for His wisdom in such leading.'[1]

What if the Schaeffers had stayed in St Louis and not gone to Europe? They could have promoted the well-being of others, led others to the Lord and served God in either place. Suppose they had stayed, what would God have done then? God would have worked with them, and accomplished His will in Europe through other people. Knowing God will work with us wherever we go in His Name and Spirit should encourage us, but does not remove our responsibility to pray for the knowledge of His will and to follow Him wherever He leads. We should not take His presence for granted and pray less than we should for His clear direction. Where we do and do not witness will make a difference. If we must choose one place over another, then, as we pray for our work, we must also pray for God to send others to give a clear testimony for Him in the place we did not choose.

What if we are asking God to send us to a specific place for a specific work, but afflictions strike and we cannot go? Did you ever stop to think what might have happened if God had literally removed all of the Apostle Paul's afflictions in answer to his prayers? What if God had removed Paul's thorn in the flesh? What if God had allowed Paul to go wherever he wanted? What if God had given Paul a greater gift of preaching to attract greater crowds wherever he travelled and had allowed people always to press around him for insights? What if God had kept Paul out of prison on various occasions? Would Paul have had the time or seen the need to dictate and write his letters? What would the Bible be like without Paul's letters? In his afflictions, the Holy Spirit inspired the Apostle Paul to do a greater work than he had done when free and well. By His grace and in spite of Paul's afflictions, God increased His influence. We learn the same principle from the prayers, brief ministry, suffering and death of Jesus Christ.

When the Lord gives us sufficient grace, as He did Paul, He promises to empower us to serve Him in His way. God's way is the only way for us to seek in prayer, and we must seek it submissively. When we do not receive from God exactly what we want, we must not assume a lot of bad things but remind ourselves that God is working out better things for us as well as others. Paul knew this, so he wrote to the Romans: 'And we know that in all things God works for the good of those who love him, who have been called according to his purpose' (Romans 8:28). God will do this in the life of every Christian. He will do this in your life and mine, as we seek to fulfil His intentions for us. Let us pray in faith for God's perfect leading and provision.

Prayer

Dear Heavenly Father, I praise You today for who You are as the Sovereign Lord of the universe. I thank You for being all-wise and powerful, and for always using Your power in the most loving and compassionate ways. Thank You for saying 'No' to me when I have prayed for the wrong things. I trust in You; help me to be a better servant and witness for Jesus' sake. Amen.

___ 2 _____

PRAYING FOR UNBELIEVERS

*Brothers, my heart's desire and prayer to God for
the Israelites is that they may be saved.*

Romans 10:1

*E*dith Schaeffer's special love for the Jews
motivated her to write *Christianity is Jewish*. And
later, when she wrote *Forever Music*, she prayed
and hoped it would help many Jewish people in
the artistic community. In answer to her prayers,
people gave copies to such legendary musicians as
Horowitz and Serkin, among others.[1] Just two

amazing stories will encourage each of us to continue praying for the Jews and look for opportunities to tell them and others about Jesus the Messiah whenever possible.

After one year in Switzerland, little Priscilla Schaeffer knew French well enough to act as a translator for prospective tenants in their boarding house. One evening, Priscilla rushed to tell her family that she had just translated from English into French so a German Jewish woman from Jerusalem could rent a room from Madame Turrian. When Fran and Edith met the woman later, she bubbled over with excitement as she spoke about the re-establishment of Israel. She told about the great expectations of those who believed God might be doing something new in their midst.

In the coming days, God used the perfect timing of these events in Israel to give her a receptive mind for what the Schaeffer family had to tell her about Jesus the Messiah. And as the time for her return to Israel approached, the Schaeffers longed to give her a gift, a special Prophecy Edition of the New Testament. However, they did not know where to find one in Switzerland, and they knew they could not send to America and get one back in time. So they prayed fervently for a Bible to give, and trusted in God as they went about their daily tasks.

A few days later, on the last afternoon of a conference, Edith heard a man from the Million Testaments Campaigns give a lecture. Afterwards, she hurried to the platform and asked him, 'Do you have a Prophecy New Testament?' He smiled, reached into his coat pocket, pulled out and gave her exactly what she wanted. What a wonderful, specific answer to their prayers.[2]

The day the Jewish woman left, the Schaeffers gave her some gifts, including the Prophecy New Testament. They showed her why she should study it, and with a glowing face she accepted the Bible and promised to read it. The Schaeffers continued to pray for her, but they never saw her again. Because of God's perfect timing for her to meet the Schaeffers and receive her Bible at that time in Israel's history, we can presume that she eventually accepted Jesus as the Messiah and her personal Saviour.

Edith learned about the other amazing answer to prayer fourteen years after she and Fran witnessed to and prayed for a woman they met in an alley. In 1978, Francis Schaeffer was working on his book and film *Whatever Happened to the Human Race?* and Edith was writing *Affliction*. On the warm sunny days in the Alps, they wrote in their back garden and socialised with the neighbours who stopped to chat over the fence. They got to know one such neighbour very well, a Jewish woman. She told them how she and her husband fled Germany in 1938 to escape the persecution. First, they went to South Africa and worked there for many years, and then they moved to Switzerland, where her husband had died. Fran and Edith told her about their faith in God. They prayed for her, and Fran gave her a copy of *The God Who is There*.[3] But after Fran began treatment for cancer in Rochester, Minnesota in late 1978, they did not think they would see her again.

In July of 1992, Edith returned to Switzerland to work with Swiss L'Abri and take a rest from her work in America. One Sunday in August, she attended an English-speaking church and after the service the pastor asked her to stay and meet a woman who had come to believe in Jesus just six months before in their church. To her amazement and delight, Edith met the Jewish woman to whom Fran had given *The God Who is There*. In answer to their many prayers, the woman told how God had motivated her to read the book, and then later how she had found and read Edith's book *L'Abri*, and then many years later she had accepted Jesus as the Messiah.[4]

Edith can tell many stories about people who have come to the Saviour in answer to their prayers and through the truths people have learned from their books. Over the years, the Holy Spirit has graciously brought people to the

Schaeffers, or got the Schaeffers' books into their hands, and then much later the Schaeffers have met these people in unexpected places and have heard their testimony.

Our prayers are one means God has ordained to use in the salvation of sinners. By His grace, God leads people to pray for those who need to know His Son. Sometimes He inspires people to pray by name for someone they know personally or for someone they have only heard about. At other times He will inspire people to pray for an opportunity to tell some known (or not yet known) person about God's provision for salvation through faith in Jesus. We might pray for these opportunities as we ride on a bus or train. Edith always does this, and God usually honours her request.

For example, a few years after Fran died, as she was flying back to America from Europe, a woman from an Arabic country called her over to her seat and angrily demanded, 'Why are you so different from everybody else?' Edith calmly explained that she looked at things differently, and before they reached America the woman had turned from being a Moslem to accepting Jesus as her Saviour. In the coming months, Edith very carefully sent her books that she hoped would get through the censors, and not get the woman arrested. And then she followed them with letters asking about specific pages in ways that would not incriminate her new Christian friend. She prayed for the Lord to protect and defend her, and open doors for her to witness safely at home. As we faithfully obey God's leading in teaching us how to pray, we will see God using us to change people's lives in many different ways, and then we may need to pray for the Lord's protection as they live out their faith.

Many times the Schaeffers saw the fruit of their prayers and teaching, and God used them personally as His harvest workers to reap the results of their labours. On other occasions, they only shared God's Word, and then watered their witness with their tears as they prayed for the individual. They always rejoiced when they learned that someone else had been able to follow through from their beginning and lead someone to receive Jesus as their Saviour and Lord. In heaven, all the faithful followers of Jesus will meet those who came to believe because they cared, prayed, shared and taught them the truth about God.

Prayer

Dear Father, thank You for loving Your people, the Jews, as a faithful Parent. Thank You for preparing them to be the nation that would teach others about Your way of salvation through the Messiah. Help me to pray for Jews and others with an understanding of how much You love them and of how much they mean to You. Help me to teach others about Your wonderful love for all peoples, and show them You have a purpose for each of our lives. Keep me from being personally offended when others challenge my Christian attitude or demeanour, and help me share with them the joy that knowing You makes, so some may come to follow You. For the sake of Jesus' Kingdom, I pray. Amen.

— 3 —————————

GOD COMFORTS IN MANY WAYS

Praise be to the God and Father of our Lord Jesus Christ, the Father of compassion and the God of all comfort, who comforts us in all our troubles, so that we can comfort those in any trouble with the comfort we ourselves have received from God . . . He has delivered us from such a deadly peril, and he will deliver us. On him we have set our hope that he will continue to deliver us, as you help us by your prayers. Then many will give thanks on our behalf for the gracious favour granted us in answer to the prayers of many.

2 Corinthians 1:3–4, 10–11

*L*ong before we ever know we will need the comfort, God often gives us the assurance of His provision by giving us examples of how He has sustained others through difficult times. For example, God can introduce us to a family with a child who has handicaps, and show us the love and wonder in his life, years before we give birth to or adopt a handicapped child. Many times God will comfort us in advance of our need, and when we look back we receive the consolation that God has worked in the past to prepare us for the present.

Sometimes God will work good in our lives through other people's difficulties. We have not caused their problems, but God brings good into our lives by allowing us to observe the good He brings to them in their afflictions. Remembering God's gracious love given to others will inspire us to trust in God at all times. Then, in *our* afflictions, we can demonstrate God's consolation and God will work good in someone else's life as well as our own. God can introduce us to a person who has overcome a great challenge or a particular temptation long before we face a similar challenge or test, so we will know what God's faithfulness and our obedience can bring in a time of trial. Sometimes God will teach us how to pray by showing us how others have prayed and He has provided. At other times, God expects us to pray for those in need and see our prayers answered, so we will learn how to pray in later times of need.

One Sunday afternoon a young American soldier visited the Schaeffers in their Swiss home. Their conversation turned to a pastor in Zurich that the young man knew personally, but the Schaeffers had never met. The pastor, who had a young family, had been voted out of his church for emphasising God's grace and some essential biblical teachings. At first, the pastor had tried some secular jobs to support his family, but God led him back into teaching the Bible in homes, travelling to other countries to preach, and supporting his family by faith through prayer. As they discussed this pastor and his problems, they answered a knock at the door and there stood this very pastor. The pastor spoke German and the American soldier interpreted so the Schaeffers could understand. Without God's perfect timing, the Schaeffers would have had great difficulty in understanding their unexpected guest or talking with him about all that needed to be said in a short period of time.

God orchestrated this encounter to help the pastor from Zurich, who needed to know that there were many others who still believed as he did, and to impress upon the Schaeffers how He could provide for a pastor and his family if they took a stand for God and truth in spite of the cost. God's lesson to the Schaeffers about courage, obedience, and prayer through this man made such an impression upon Edith that when she wrote home she asked people to pray for him. Years before they would ever need this lesson and the comfort it would bring in a time of uncertainty and trial, God brought this pastor to the Schaeffers' home to teach them more about the power of prayer.

When we think carefully about God going before us in our own lives, we may remember similar instances of God's provision of comfort and guidance in advance. We can take comfort from God's faithfulness to the Apostle Paul and the early martyrs in meeting their needs, but God will also teach us from the lives of our contemporaries. Just as the Schaeffers learned from others, they can be contemporary examples for us regarding effective prayer and trying to do practical things to help others.

The Schaeffer family eventually decided to live by prayer and faith alone in 1955, because they faced continuing conflict in their denomination over Fran's teaching on sanctification and some other theological questions. The mission board cut their meagre missionary salary, so they had to decide whether they would continue their missionary work as a venture of faith, go back to America or do something else with their lives. In

1949, six years before they founded L'Abri in the midst of a crisis, God demonstrated to them through a Zurich pastor that He could provide for their needs and the needs of others simply through prayer and through their obedience in the work that He wanted done. Our God is a good and gracious Master who takes care of His servants by anticipating their needs, whatever they may be.

As we speak to others, whether they are Christians or not, God will teach us valuable lessons. Some of these lessons will be for the future. We need to pray for nonbelievers to receive the truths we share, and also for God to teach us what He wants us to learn from and through them. As we talk to believers who have suffered for their faith or who have faced severe health or financial problems, we need to learn from them all we can about God's faithfulness and His answers to prayer. If we never face similar afflictions, if we prepare ourselves to serve God according to His leading, we will be able to help some by telling them inspirational stories of God's faithfulness to others. As we pray for opportunities to tell others about God, we need to look for God to answer us in ways that will involve far more than simply telling them some theological facts or quoting some Bible verses. In every case, we need to pray for God's Holy Spirit to show us what to share and how, in order to make our testimony effective.

Edith asked others to pray for their new friend in the ministry, and the Schaeffers learned to depend on the prayers of many people to help them do their work. They did not take the prayers of others for granted, but praised God that others who lived far away could enter into their work with them through prayer. We will never rise above the need for the prayers of others, and our prayers for others will benefit them in more ways than just giving them a psychological lift. Our prayers will often free God's hand to work in their lives according to the principles He has established when people pray.

The Apostle Paul wrote that he depended upon the prayers of the Corinthians, and that their prayers had delivered him on many occasions. When we ask others to pray for us, we need to encourage them by telling them how God has heard their prayers in our times of need. Paul did this to encourage the Corinthians to keep on praying, and we can do the same today. If we stop and appreciate what God is doing in our work, we will praise Him before others and that will motivate them to keep constant in prayer and look for more opportunities to intercede for others.

Prayer

Dear Jesus, help me learn all I can about You by observing Your work in the lives of others as well as my own. I praise You for being unchanging and always consistent, so I can see how You apply the principles and promises I have learned from Your Word in the lives of others. In every case where I suffer, help me to bring great blessing to others by showing them the power of Your work in my life in the midst of tribulation. Amen.

— 4 —

GOD HAS PROVIDED BEFORE WE PRAY

> *But when you pray, go into your room, close the door and pray to your Father, who is unseen. Then your Father, who sees what is done in secret, will reward you. And when you pray, do not keep on babbling like pagans, for they think they will be heard because of their many words. Do not be like them, for your Father knows what you need before you ask him.*
>
> Matthew 6:6–8

When they first arrived in Switzerland, Fran, Edith, Priscilla, Susan and Debby lived in two small rooms in Madame Turrian's boarding house in Lausanne. Edith continued to pray that people would once again hear Fran teach the Bible, but she had no idea how God would answer her prayers. They converted one of their bedrooms into a temporary sanctuary, and began Sunday services for their family. They sang hymns, took an offering for other missionaries, and Fran preached a full sermon. God began to answer Edith's prayers when a little Irish woman, who also lived in the boarding house, began to attend their services regularly.

As winter turned to spring, Madame Wildermuth, their French teacher, became concerned about the girls' health and convinced the Schaeffers to spend the summer in the mountains. As their summer in the Alps neared an end, they wondered if they might be able to stay in Chalet Bon Accueil in Champéry for the full year. As they prayed, Edith carefully figured their finances and they looked for a school for the girls. After knowing what they could spend and that schooling could be arranged, they prayed very specifically: 'Dear Heavenly Father, if it is Thy will for us to be here *this* year, the Marclays [from whom they rented Chalet Bon Accueil] could easily get word changing the plans and freeing this chalet, or perhaps there is another chalet suitable for us. Please show us Thy will.'[1]

When the Schaeffers prayed to stay in Champéry, they gave God some good and unselfish reasons for staying. In their larger home in Champéry, God had led them to teach the Bible to some of the girls who came to Switzerland for school or on vacation, and they needed this larger home to teach more people. If they stayed, this work with these and other girls could continue. They had also discussed truth and the Bible with others who had travelled to their home, so it was not out of the way. From this new location, they could still travel easily to Finland, Holland, England and other places to promote Children For Christ. But as they prayed, they also wanted to be fair with Madame Turrian, since they had told her they would return in the autumn. They wanted God to help her to find new tenants and not lose the income she needed.

The whole family prayed that God would answer their prayers by the Friday before they needed to leave. When Friday came, they had received no answer. With downcast hearts, they walked into the village to say goodbye. As they neared the hotel, Madame Wildermuth's sister met them and indicated that her brother might let them another home, Chalet des Frênes, in Champéry for a year, for less than he would let it for the four months during the summer and winter vacations. After asking him the price, Madame Wildermuth thought the Lord must have put the amount in his mind: he gave them such a low rate they could afford to stay.

A wealthy English lady had built Chalet des Frênes about twenty years earlier, while Edith was still at school in Canada. As she went from room to room, Edith discovered that her decorating tastes must have been similar to hers. Could the Lord have been providing this home for them even before they had prayed for it?

The Schaeffers went back to Lausanne and returned to Champéry in November. Just before Christmas a French-speaking minister asked Pastor Schaeffer to provide a Christmas Eve service in English for the Protestant Church in Champéry. Prior to World War I, another English lady had built a chapel for Protestant worship (especially for the English-speaking tourists) in this Roman Catholic canton. She had built it near the train station for everyone to see, and had included Scripture texts on the inside walls as a silent testimony to the gospel. On Christmas Sunday, Fran preached to about 150 worshippers, including girls from England and boys from Scotland. Following the service, he learned that he could conduct weekly services in the church for as long as they lived in Champéry. What an answer to Edith's prayers! Within two years from the time they left America, Francis Schaeffer was preaching 'in a real church' again, and he continued to conduct Christmas Eve services in that church for the next thirty-two years. Years before they needed a home in the Alps and a church in which to preach, the Lord had provided for their needs.

When we pray and ask others to pray for us, we never know whose prayers are being answered as God works in our lives. As we think of the hopes and prayers of the English woman who built her chapel in 1912 (the year Fran was born), we do not know if Francis Schaeffer preached there in answer to her prayers offered thirty or forty years earlier, or in answer to the Schaeffers' prayers, or in answer to all their prayers and the prayers of others combined. In this life, the combination of God's purposes and our prayers remains a mystery. God teaches us, however, that what we do right now—what we pray, build, say or write—might meet the needs of some unknown person or group tens or hundreds of years in the future. By praying for the Lord's leading and plan, and by doing the very best we can *today* for His glory, our work can benefit countless numbers of people over an unforeseen number of years.

The Schaeffers really prayed for God to use them fully in any way that He chose. They were careful stewards of the Lord's money. They took nothing for granted, but praised God for His many answers to their prayers. They continued to pray for God's direction, and asked others to pray with them regarding very specific people and things. As they sought God's guidance, they considered the concerns and needs of others, and prayed and planned carefully so that others might not be adversely affected in answer to their prayers. They did not want to give God any good reasons for saying 'No' to their requests.

Jesus encourages us to pray by saying that our Heavenly Father knows our needs even before we pray. He inspires us to persevere in prayer by telling us that God has provided for our needs in advance. Yet, in some mysterious way, many of God's provisions depend upon our prayers. As we converse with God, we discover God's leading. Through prayer and fellowship with God, we learn to follow God and go to the people and places He has prepared for us in advance. God builds our faith by answering our specific prayers. We see Him going on ahead of us, leading us, guiding us, providing for us, and strengthening our faith in Him.

Prayer

Dear Heavenly Father, teach me the lessons You want me to learn from these answered prayers of the Schaeffers. Help me to see that You love and care for me just as much as You love and care for others. Help me to see how much You do for me each day, so I can praise You each day for Your wonderful provisions. Help me to be more specific in my prayers as I seek to know and do Your will. Help me to glorify Your name in all I pray and do. Help me to show and teach others how You want us to pray. Amen.

5

LEARNING TO PRAY

One day Jesus was praying in a certain place. When he finished, one of his disciples said to him, 'Lord, teach us to pray, just as John taught his disciples.'

Luke 11:1

*E*ven before they founded L'Abri, the Schaeffers lived by prayer and depended on the prayers of others to help them show forth the glory of God and lead others to faith in Him. Because some people recognised their closeness to God, their life of prayer, and God's continual faithfulness to them, they wanted the Schaeffers to teach them about God and prayer. Before they moved, Madame Turrian had known the Schaeffers long enough to see God work in their lives and solve their problems, so she asked them to teach her how to pray.

First, Fran and Edith pointed her to Jesus Christ, and His willingness to answer the prayers of those who placed their faith in Him alone as their Saviour. They assured her that God had pledged Himself to answer the prayers of believers in Jesus, of those who prayed in His name. They showed her in the Bible how God answered the many prayers of His people and met their daily needs. They told her to pray and read the Scriptures to learn why God answers the prayers of His people, and said that the more she prayed, the more the Holy Spirit would teach her about prayer.

When Madame Turrian learned that the Schaeffers wanted to live in the mountains and not return to her boarding house, she became concerned about the income she needed each month. Of course the Schaeffers had already been praying about this, but they encouraged her to pray as well, to see what God could do for her in answer to her prayers. In this time of her own need, Madame Turrian began to learn that God wanted her to trust in Him and not the Schaeffers' prayers or other tenants to meet her needs. God wanted her to learn that He loved her and would hear her prayers too.

Like so many new believers, Madame Turrian prayed, but also set the conditions that she wanted God to fulfil in answering her prayers. She did not want to release the Schaeffers from their rental agreement until every room they had used had been let. She prayed for God to meet her needs, but within the predetermined boundaries she set. And then, as she prayed and read her Bible, God taught her more about faith and surrender. She learned that she needed to surrender her life to God and His loving care with a deeper trust in His wisdom. She needed to trust that God would provide for her in His way, and that His way would be the best way for everyone. She needed to surrender her will to God, and pray, 'Not as I will, but as you will' (Matthew 26:39). Because God wanted to teach her this next lesson in prayer, He would not bring her tenants until she surrendered her will to His. But at the same time, by His grace and Spirit, God knew that He could teach her this lesson in time for the Schaeffers to move to the mountains so Fran could preach at a Christmas Eve service they knew nothing about yet.

In addition to praying, the Schaeffers made an effort to find tenants for Madame Turrian. And then, just before they needed to move, God revealed the problem to Madame Turrian. She went to Edith and said, 'I believe that the Lord wants me to be willing not to let them, to stop saying that they must be let.'[1] Edith and Madame Turrian prayed again, and the very next day tenants came to rent her rooms. Madame Turrian and the Schaeffers rejoiced to see God's wonderful provision for all their needs and His perfect timing.

Teaching others to pray in these practical ways began almost the very moment the Schaeffers moved to Switzerland. After they founded L'Abri, Edith taught many times on prayer, especially on their days of prayer and special days of fasting.[2] She encouraged the members, workers, helpers, and students at L'Abri to persevere in prayer by telling of the many answers to prayer they and others had received at L'Abri. Her inspirational examples of answered prayer poured out one after the other until they all dismissed for prayer. And because the Schaeffers maintained a constant closeness to God in prayer, their stories of God's answers to prayer were not all from the distant past. They told about the things God was doing in the present, and asked for prayers that today's needs be met, so students and nonbelievers at L'Abri could see for themselves that God existed and answered prayers. They knew and taught that

God is consistent and answers prayer today according to His unchanging principles in the Bible.

Before God led them to trust so totally in prayer for Him to meet their needs and those they served in L'Abri, God taught them how to teach others about prayer. Just as Jesus' disciples recognised His closeness to His Heavenly Father and asked Him to teach them how to pray, so many who came to know the Schaeffers asked them to teach them about God and prayer. God wants us to learn everything we can about His grace, faithfulness, and desire to hear prayer from the biographies of His servants, so we can learn how to pray more effectively from them and by experience. And as we learn, God will give us opportunities to teach others about Jesus and how to pray as He has commanded.

Throughout their prayers, the Schaeffers demonstrated submission or surrender to God, putting His will before theirs. They prayed for God's Kingdom to come and then worked and witnessed so others would enter His Kingdom. They prayed for God's will to be done, and then sought to understand and obey God's clear pronouncements or commands in the Scriptures. They prayed for God's will to be done, and then for the courage and wisdom to do His will in specific situations. God wants to teach us these principles, not just so we can pray for Him to meet our needs, but so His meeting our needs will bless others too.

The Schaeffers saw their personal needs in the context of following Jesus, so they prayed for God's provision in the context of what would help them demonstrate the glory of God and bless others. This seems to be the open secret of their effective prayers. God honoured the spirit of their prayers and taught them the right priorities in prayer. Those who spent much time with them learned the fundamental principle of submission from their lives and manner of praying.

As God teaches us how to pray for our needs, He will lead us to be submissive in prayer. Our prayers will not be as effective as God wants them to be until we learn this lesson. If our prayers seem ineffective, we may have allowed our needs to take precedence over God's purposes. Our sincere confession of this selfishness and a firm resolve to live for God by His grace will often free His hand to bless us in ways that would otherwise be impossible or inconsistent with His holy character. Sometimes, we need to ask God to show us any barriers that we have set up that are preventing His answers, because we might not be as submissive to Him as we think.

Prayer

Dear Jesus, in my times of greatest need, I sometimes spend more time asking for my need to be met than seeking Your will in my situation. Teach me to be submissive to You in all things. Teach me to pray for Your will to be done before all else. Give me the confidence I need to believe that You know far better than I exactly what I need. If I am blind to a sin that is preventing Your answering my prayers, show me what I need to confess and change to honour You and receive the blessing I seek. Amen.

6

PRAYING FOR NEW THINGS

What other nation is so great as to have their gods near them the way the LORD our God is near us whenever we pray to him?

Deuteronomy 4:7

When we are far away from family and old friends, we tend to trust more in the Lord than when we can easily reach out to someone who understands and will care for us in time of need. As they promoted Children For Christ and fought Modernism and Barthianism wherever they travelled, the Schaeffers went to many different countries in Europe. In their early years, they had great difficulties travelling because each country's language was foreign to them. In many situations they could not talk to anyone else about their needs. So, God taught them to bring everything to Him in prayer. God allowed them to get into situations where only He could help, and then in answer to their prayers He delivered them time and time again. In this way, God strengthened their faith and taught them never to take His care for granted, but to praise Him in all things and every time He rescued them.

One day when they were travelling, Fran left his camera on the train and only remembered its loss when it sped off towards Helsinki. He and Edith asked the people on the platform for help, but no one understood them. They knew only one Person could help, so they prayed and asked God to reveal Fran's camera to their former travelling companion who had stayed on the train. They prayed specifically that he would see the camera hanging behind some women's coats and send it back to them. The situation seemed impossible, but they knew that God could retrieve a camera which they could not afford to lose. As they waited at the station for their next train, Edith heard 'Schaeffer' announced over the loud-speakers, but in the context of a foreign language that had no meaning to them. They heard it again, but could not understand what it meant; so they went to the telegraph office and learned that their friend had indeed found Fran's camera and would send it back on the next train. Fran and Edith rejoiced that God had heard their prayers once again.

God wants us to share everything with Him. None of our concerns are too unimportant or insignificant from His point of view. God shows His great love for us by teaching us to talk with Him about every single thing, great and small. As our best Friend, He wants to draw us closer and keep us in continual conversation. As we get to know our great Friend better, we learn that we must take everything to Him in prayer. As we love God more and more, we will naturally (or better, *supernaturally*) want to be with Him and keep talking to Him no matter what we are doing, while we are doing it, and wherever we are going.

God also taught the Schaeffers that living by faith and prayer does not mean that we will never face deep hurts and losses. Living by faith and prayer does not prevent us from experiencing the consequences of living in a fallen world: the sins of others and the results of nature's brokenness will injure us. We do not know why Fran could lose a camera and then have it returned in answer to prayer; and then, a short time later, why they would pray and Edith would still lose their unborn baby and almost her life with the complications. 'Aren't babies more valuable than cameras?' we might ask. If God can return a camera, can't He see a child safely from conception through birth? Yes, God can. When He does not, He has still promised believers in His Word that He will give them the grace they need in all things and will work everything that happens for their good and His glory. God has a purpose for our lives, and all our trials have a part. Sometimes, even in this life, God will allow us to see some of the blessings He brings from our troubles.

God led the Schaeffers through many traumatic afflictions and battles with demonic forces, because if they were going to use faith and prayer to demonstrate His reality, He would have to demonstrate His love, power, and all-sufficient grace in many varied circumstances—including great losses. Living by faith is no guarantee we will not have difficulties. The commitment to live by faith alone may only guarantee that we will have to face trials and troubles that others may never face, so God can demonstrate in an authentic way His character, wisdom and might in many difficult situations.

In His Beatitudes, Jesus described seven wonderful blessings that will result from following

Him and allowing Him to develop His character within us, and then He ended with the eighth promised blessing that if we are righteous and follow Him we may receive insults, persecutions, and false accusations (see Matthew 5:1–12). As God improved their character, the Schaeffers experienced all of these things in Switzerland. From the beginning of their mission work, they learned how Satan could oppose them by using the government and people who professed to be Christians.

Living a life of faith does not guarantee an easy time. An easy time does not guarantee we are living by faith. A particularly dark period in our lives may not indicate that we have forsaken God, but that Satan is attacking our hearts and minds, and that we are still being faithful. If we do not learn this lesson early in our walk with the Lord, we may give up or misunderstand His leading when temptations and troubles pour in upon us.

With the loss of their baby and Edith's subsequent need to slow down and get a complete rest for her health, God taught her a new lesson on prayer. In the past, she had always prayed for more strength or time to get the needed work done herself. She remembered times when God simply 'stopped their mail' for a time when they were all sick and did not want to get behind in their correspondence. But this time, God taught Edith to pray for some people to help her. As she rested in bed and read her Bible, she began to ask God to provide someone who could take Fran's dictation. In the morning, she once again surrendered herself and her important work to God, *for Him to set her aside for ever if necessary,* for His provision of the help they needed if possible. And that very day she received a confirmation letter and phone call that God had provided suitable help. Almost immediately after God taught her this lesson and she submitted to His will, He provided just what they needed. Fran received the help of an executive secretary so that Edith could rest.

In every affliction, we can trust God to teach us something about prayer and His character that will help us and others. If we do not fall to the temptation of blaming God, or of accusing God for being insensitive to our needs, or of becoming angry with God for not putting His awesome power at our personal disposal whenever we need it, then God will explain to us through His Word or in other ways the lessons we can learn in our situation for our benefit and that of others. If we remain faithful, God will always answer the spirit of our prayers and give us what we really need.

Prayer

Dear God, as I study prayer, I do not know why some prayers are answered and some are not. But I do trust in Your holy character; in Your love, justice, mercy, grace and fairness. I know that You will work out all things for good. Please help me live each day on this belief and share this truth with others in ways that may be of real help to them. In Jesus' name, Amen.

— 7 ——————

LIVING BY FAITH

*No one can serve two masters. Either he will hate
the one and love the other, or he will be devoted to
the one and despise the other. You cannot serve
both God and Money. Therefore I tell you, do not
worry about your life, what you will eat or drink;
or about your body, what you will wear. Is not
life more important than food, and the body more
important than clothes? Look at the birds of the
air; they do not sow or reap or store away in
barns, and yet your heavenly Father feeds them.
Are you not much more valuable than they?*

Matthew 6:24–26

*I*f we work forty hours per week and get a regular pay cheque, God still calls us to live by faith. If we have a traditional job, we should thank God for a job and steady income, and also trust God and pray for His daily provisions as the Lord's Prayer teaches. If we are laid off, fired, or our company closes, and we do not know where our next job will be or when our next pay cheque will come, perhaps we trust in God with greater desperation, but trust in God we must.

Living by faith can also have a different meaning. A house painter, paper hanger, artist or musician may only pray for work and never advertise their services or product to the general public. Another person may pray for work and God's guidance on where and how he will advertise and how much he will spend to promote his product. Neither way is necessarily more spiritual than the other way. Only God can determine who is living more by faith than someone else. Each person may be living equally by faith alone, allowing the Holy Spirit to lead them. Faith involves trust. Faith includes believing the Scriptures and following God according to the best understanding we have regarding God and what He wants us to do personally. Usually, faith does not mean simply doing exactly what God has led someone we admire to do; but it can, if we are certain that God is calling us to follow in their footsteps. Learning from the example of someone's consistent Christian character is usually far wiser than trying to be a doctor only because some Christian we know is a highly successful surgeon. Only after an evaluation of God's providential work in our lives and much prayer for His guidance should we go into any kind of work or ministry.

Ordinarily, when we think of living by faith, we think of missionaries, evangelists, pastors and revivalists who trust solely in God for their food, clothing, shelter and other needs, rather than relying on a church or missionary society to give them a regular salary. When the Schaeffers founded L'Abri in 1955, God called them to a new way of living by faith *for them*. However, before God called them to take this step of faith, He providentially taught them some lessons about prayer and gave them the courage to rely on Him alone and those God moved in answer to prayer to provide for them.

The Schaeffers first went to Switzerland with a small steady salary under the sponsorship of an American mission board. But after seven years, God led them to begin living by faith alone after the model of Hudson Taylor and the China Inland Mission.[1] Eventually, God would demonstrate through them and L'Abri that He could work through the faithful prayers of His people in the same way in the twentieth century as He had in the past. We glimpse a part of God's training for a life of prayer when we see how early God began to prepare Edith and Francis Schaeffer for their life's work.

Edith Schaeffer was not *accidentally* born in China, to parents who lived by faith as missionaries in Hudson Taylor's China Inland Mission. God taught Edith before her earliest remembrance about how He could provide for a believer's needs in answer to prayer. God's providential preparation of Edith included the Holy Spirit placing the desire in her heart to accompany Dr Hoste, who succeeded Hudson Taylor as the director of CIM, as he prayed for all the missionaries under his care by name. After admonishing her not to talk as they walked, he took little four-year-old Edith by the hand as he prayed out loud for the mission's needs and the definite needs of each missionary and their children. Edith heard Dr Hoste pray for her specifically, and then she saw his prayers answered on her behalf. She heard others praising God for the answers to prayer that she had heard Dr Hoste pray about earlier, and she praised Him too. Some of her earliest recollections include hearing her parents pray and seeing God answer them in special ways. Very early in life, God impressed Edith's heart and mind with truths about His faithfulness and His desire to hear and answer our prayers.

After Fran became a Christian, God began to teach him that He could be trusted in times of need by answering his prayers as a teenager. When God called him to the ministry, Fran discovered that he would have to prepare for the work without parental encouragement and support. Since his parents were not Christians, they wanted Fran in a respectable secular job. When Fran chose to go to college and study for the ministry, Fran's father fought his decision and forced Fran to choose between God and his family. Fran would have to trust in God alone for His provision of funds for tuition and other expenses. Only after Fran declared to his earthly father that he first had to obey his Heavenly Father did his dad announce that he would help his son financially in college. Because of Fran's willingness to trust in God alone for His college provisions and because his parents saw Fran and Edith's consistent Christian living over a long period of time, they finally came to trust in Jesus as their Lord and Saviour.

From the beginning of Fran's Christian life, God began preparing him to live by faith and prayer. God showed Fran that He could move an unbeliever, his own dad, as well as believers to accomplish His purposes. God taught Fran through his own experience that He would faithfully care for any young person who needed to choose between God and his family if forced to by his parents. This early lesson encouraged Fran whenever he told others about their need for absolute loyalty to Jesus, the Lord over all, no matter what the cost. Fran knew by experience that the love and power of his Heavenly Father would be with them through everything.

As we think about our past, we need to look for instances of God's providential care and provision—enough to build up our faith in Him and convince us that we live in a supernatural world where prayer makes a difference as God works in history. We may not be called to the same type of work or to living by faith in the ways of Hudson Taylor or Francis and Edith Schaeffer. If we try to live exactly as they did without God's clear call, we may be disobeying and tempting God. Jesus pointed out to Satan, when Satan tempted Him to jump off a pinnacle and expect God to catch Him, that we can tempt God by trying to live by faith in a way that God has not called us to follow. Hence, some supposed living by faith can actually be disobedience.

Prayer

Dear Father, as I think about Your work in

my life, help me to recognise Your definite leading through the years. Help me to see and appreciate what You have been doing to prepare me for saving faith, for this present moment, and for what lies ahead. As I seek to put You first and love You more each day, help me to understand how the Scriptures relate to my deepest concerns and to living by faith for You today. For Jesus' sake, Amen.

8

PASSING ON OUR FAITH

I pray that you may be active in sharing your faith, so that you will have a full understanding of every good thing we have in Christ.

Philemon 6

We can influence others to practise our sinful habits, but we can also pass on our faith. Edith's parents passed the prayer principles and life of faith they learned from Hudson Taylor's China Inland Mission on to her. And the Holy Spirit worked in Edith's life from such an early age that

she cannot remember when she first believed in
Jesus as her Saviour. She passed on this heritage to
her children. And Priscilla, Susan and Debby
passed on their faith to their children. Some of
Edith's grandchildren now work as missionaries.
For example, one now serves with her husband in
Nepal through a Canadian missionary society. We
can easily trace four generations of missionaries
from Edith Schaeffer's parents to her grandchildren, because each generation practised their
faith and taught God's Word to their children.

Francis Schaeffer could have passed on the
unbelief and cynicism of his parents. But after
reading the Bible for himself as a teenager, he
committed his life to serving Jesus Christ. And he
too passed on his faith to the next generations. We
need not remain in the downward spiral of sin. We
can come to Jesus Christ for transformation, and
ask the Holy Spirit to help us pass on the truth of
God, instead of our sins, to our children. But we
must not take the teaching of true faith for granted.
It is possible for some in every generation to turn
from the faith of their parents.

Eventually, the Schaeffers' L'Abri became a
second generation China Inland Mission. But God
added the new element of making L'Abri into *a
spiritual orphanage* for wandering young people and
adults from all over the world. As we shall see,
with some modifications, God made L'Abri into a

combination of the work of Hudson Taylor and George Müller (the founder of Müller Homes for Children in Bristol, England).[1] Fran and Edith accomplished with their own family what they would later accomplish in what became the larger L'Abri family. Should the Lord tarry, He may raise up a third and fourth generation of fellowships and societies similar to their 'parents', but with differences that are vital for meeting the needs of each generation.

God united the Schaeffer family in the cause of serving Jesus Christ. Their great power in prayer came from this family unity. Even before L'Abri began, Priscilla, Susan and Debby committed themselves to evangelism and teaching others the Bible as much as their parents. And Fran and Edith prayed with their children for God to put the people who needed to hear the good news in their path, so that they could help them in their special ways. And then they actively looked for the people God would send them.

As Fran prayed and travelled in 1951, he witnessed for the first time to the first adult man in Champéry eventually to become a Christian through their ministry. The man knew about Schaeffer and simply asked, 'What is the difference between Roman Catholicism and Protestantism anyway?'[2] Fran's answer led to several other conversations and Bible studies, and in 1952 Mr

Exhenry prayed in his own simple way, 'I am a sinner, I believe in Jesus as my Saviour. Thank You God for sending Jesus to die for me.'[3] He later became one of the first elders in their new congregation when they formed the International Presbyterian Church.

Priscilla knew the Bible so well by the age of eleven that she talked intelligently about Christianity with an American college student travelling through Europe on the train. She made the Bible so interesting that the student received a fresh appreciation for God's Word and wanted to read the Bible and seek God's truth for herself when she got home. Later, when Priscilla attended boarding school, she habitually read her Bible before bed time, and then the other girls in her room asked her read it out loud. One evening, during 14-year-old Priscilla's reading, the Holy Spirit moved a 16-year-old German girl to stop her so she could bow her head and ask Jesus to be her Saviour.

Susan actively recruited her girl friends in the village to come to the Children For Christ classes that Priscilla taught in French, and everyone rejoiced each time Susan convinced another little girl's mother to let her attend their classes.

Debby learned to do these things from her mother and sisters. Her mother taught her a deep love for Jesus as they sang hymns together naturally, rejoicing over what the Lord was doing in their lives, when they worked together at home.

God gave the Schaeffers unity in prayer and filled their home with a joyful love for people. Through daily prayer, hymn singing, reading *Daily Light*, and family worship, they maintained their joy in the Lord.[4] They studied their Bibles personally and prayed privately each day. And then God opened the eyes of others, and they saw such joy in the Schaeffers that they were drawn to them and asked about the God they worshipped. Girls from India in boarding school, who knew about Hinduism and Roman Catholicism personally, saw such a radiance in the Schaeffers that they were drawn to their home to study the Bible and ask questions. Some of these girls accepted Christ as their Saviour and went home to witness for Him in spite of the rejection and persecution of their families. The new reality of Christ's joy in their hearts was so real that they could return home and suffer in His name.

Because Fran and Edith encouraged the entire family to share their faith actively with others, God taught them more and more about the good things of Jesus Christ. As they learned more, they could meet the needs of more people, and they had more to share with others. They prayed for each other to be given the opportunity to witness, and they also prepared themselves spiritually and intellectually so that they would have something real and meaningful to teach. Through daily prayer, they remained close to the Lord so that His joy would fill them and overflow to others. Through prayer, the Holy Spirit showed them deeper truths from the Bible so that they could teach what they learned to others. Because they prayed fervently and worshipped the Lord together each day, biblical truths remained fresh and alive in their minds, and the Holy Spirit enabled them to lead others to the Saviour.

Through much prayer, God will change us and use us more effectively; and then our prayer requests will more consistently reflect His loving and holy character. As we strive to grow in our faith and pass on truth to our children, they must see us actively practising our faith. If we teach about prayer, our lives must show the importance of prayer. If we teach about witnessing, we must be witnessing. If we talk about sin, we must confess and forsake sin. Our children will learn about God by our prayers, words and actions. But if we seek to pass our faith on to others, even to our own children, some may still turn away and we will be grieved; however, we are not necessarily the failures if some refuse to believe and come to the Saviour.

Prayer

Dear Jesus, You died for my sins and saved my soul, and then You cleansed me and filled me with Your Spirit. Help me teach others the truths about You that they need to hear. Amen.

— 9 —

GOD SAVES THROUGH THE TRUTH

As for me, far be it from me that I should sin against the LORD by failing to pray for you. And I will teach you the way that is good and right.

1 Samuel 12:23

*T*he Schaeffers never expected to convert anyone by prayer alone or truth alone. They prayed for unbelievers, but always so that they or someone else could teach the truth to them in ways they

85

would accept. The Holy Spirit uses the truth of God and Christians as the means for saving sinners; so, God teaches us to pray for the Holy Spirit to do His work in His way in us and others. And when we open our lives to the Holy Spirit's leading, He teaches us who to pray for, and how to pray for and share the truth with them.

We need to pray for the Holy Spirit to show us what specific truths the other person needs to hear to be saved or have their questions answered. We need to pray for the Holy Spirit to give us the right spirit as we share the truth. We need to pray for the Holy Spirit to reveal the truth, holiness and love of Jesus through us in a way that will influence unbelievers to bow before Him and give Him their lives. We need to pray for the Holy Spirit to empower all new believers to live daily according to the truths of the Bible and overcome sin and temptations. In answer to prayer, God will often reveal to us the exact needs of others, so we can pray precisely for those needs and not just for needs in general.

The prophet Samuel considered it a sin if he failed to pray for those in his care or if he failed to teach them the good and right way. God placed this same obligation upon Francis and Edith Schaeffer, and they accepted this responsibility. And then the Holy Spirit sometimes gave them foresight or knowledge into the needs of others that seems almost prophetic. Sometimes they would pray out loud for people, and the Holy Spirit would move them to pray specifically about their unspoken needs. We will never have great power in prayer until we take upon ourselves this same obligation that God has revealed to every Christian through the prophet Samuel. Certainly, if we are filled with the Spirit, we will have the same attitude and sense of responsibility for others that he had.

Many have been prayed for and not converted, because some Christians have not shared the truth of God with them or prayed for God to give them the opportunity to do so. Others have not been saved because even though the truth has been taught, Christians have not prayed for the right truth to share at the right time in the right spirit, and for the Holy Spirit (who understands the working of each person's mind) to apply the truth in the way that will lead to salvation. The right truths taught in the wrong way, or in the wrong spirit, or without love, or without sufficient prayer can harden the sinner's heart and make it more difficult later to lead them to the Saviour. The Schaeffers helped many gospel-hardened sinners come to the Saviour by praying for the Holy Spirit to work all the right elements together as they shared the truth with them.

As much as they loved others, the Schaeffers

knew they needed to please God more than man; so they did not try to please people by withholding biblical truths that some might consider unpleasant. As they spoke about the exclusive claims of Jesus Christ, and said that He was the only way to the Father, the Holy Spirit revealed a supernatural joy and love that attracted some instead of repelling them. The Holy Spirit made an authentic difference in the Schaeffers' lives through His truth and their prayers, and this influenced some to turn from atheism and other religions to Jesus Christ. If they had not spent much time in prayer and Bible study, some would never have asked questions in their home and seriously considered the Bible's answers.

The Schaeffer family prayed that everything they did would show forth the glory and holiness of God. They prayed that their everyday decisions and behaviour would demonstrate the reality of God's involvement in our world. When they began their work in Switzerland, they could have taken what some believe is the only kind approach and not spoken the truth about the only way to heaven—by grace through faith in Jesus Christ. They could have lied, by not telling *the whole truth* about Jesus' teachings about Himself, or they could have cut out of their message those things in the Bible that they knew would displease the unbelieving sinner. However, the Schaeffers strove for complete honesty and opposed the methods and teaching of a liberal theology that tried to accommodate itself to every person and religion. Instead, they prayed that God would help them speak the truth in the most kind and loving way they could. When a Jew, Hindu or Moslem asked them about Christianity, they could have tried to be tolerant and said nice things about these religions, but instead they spoke the truth with love and showed concern for the person.

The Schaeffer family knew that much prayer would be needed for the Holy Spirit's leading and power, if they were to show forth the love of God for sinners through their lives and words as they spoke to non-Christians. As Fran preached or answered questions, Edith and the girls prayed for the Holy Spirit to make Fran and his words effective in the conversion of sinners. They considered their prayers a real part of this work. Their faithfulness both in prayer and speaking the truth boldly in love enabled God to use them more effectively than many others, and makes them an example for us.

We need to remember that speaking the truth is the kindest thing we can do, so we need to pray that God will help us do so kindly. When we speak the truth about Jesus, we are speaking about the One who died for sinners with a broken heart of love for them. When we speak the truth about

Jesus, we are teaching people how they too can have eternal life—the greatest gift that God can give through us. But if we speak with an unkind spirit as we teach about a way that seems to many so unkind, Satan may blind them to the very kindness of God which can lead to salvation. Only much prayer, for the Holy Spirit to help us be kind and bold at the same time, will make our witnessing effective for many.

After some of the girls who visited Fran and Edith were led to the Saviour, they took on the same loving concern for the lost that they saw in the Schaeffer family. When Mr Exhenry came to the Saviour, he wanted his whole family to hear the good news and he tried to make them interested in Jesus Christ. The Schaeffers' witnessing led believers to be remade in the image of Christ, and to their consciously choosing to take on the Christ-like spirit and characteristics they saw modelled for them in the Schaeffer family. Our tasks and their possible consequences are awesome to contemplate, and when we see the enormity of our responsibilities, we are driven to praying for others and to teaching as many as possible the good and right way through our words and actions.

Prayer

Dear Heavenly Father, as I think about the answers to prayer that the Schaeffer family received, help me to praise You and marvel at Your love. But keep me from walking away from my reading about prayer and not practising prayer as I ought. I do pray for Your Holy Spirit to place Your burden for the lost on my heart, and to teach me how I can reach them with the talents that You have given me. In Jesus' name. Amen.

—— 10 ——

WHEN GOD MOVES SLOWLY

Finally, brothers, pray for us that the message of the Lord may spread rapidly and be honoured, just as it was with you.

2 Thessalonians 3:1

After the Schaeffers moved to Champéry in 1949, Dr Otten became their family doctor and friend. He was an unbeliever, and did not have the time to attend Bible studies or talk much with Fran about Christianity. He did not see the value of spiritual concerns as he carried on his busy practice.

However, something about the Schaeffer family drew him to them, and his highly intelligent mind began to appreciate Fran's wisdom and approach to faith.

The whole family began praying for Dr Otten and asked God to help them find a way to reach him with the truth. Finally, Fran thought of asking Dr Otten if he would read some Bible studies that he would write personally for him, so he could read them at his convenience rather than coming to his home for weekly Bible studies. Dr Otten agreed; so Edith typed them and Fran delivered them to his office. Then the Holy Spirit began to move on Dr Otten as he studied Fran's lessons, but he made no commitment to Christ.

As time passed, he got to know the Schaeffer family better. He saw how they cared for the villagers and the foreign students attending the schools around them. He learned they cared much like a doctor would care for his patients. They not only shared their faith, but they practised their faith by helping the needy. From some of the villagers, he learned about the Christmas Eve when the Schaeffers had taken a complete American Christmas dinner to an old woman who lived in small, draughty, broken-down chalet and lived only on bread and cheese. She was amazed to see foods that she had never eaten before and kept asking, 'Is this for me? Is this for me?' They explained the meaning of Jesus' birth, and told her the meal was a gift from God to her for Christmas. As Dr Otten learned about their expressions of love in the village, he began to take Fran's lessons more seriously. He treated them more as friends, but chose not to follow Christ.

After more than two years, the truth they shared and the example they set influenced Dr Otten to come to their home for a serious after-dinner discussion with Fran. Edith needed to leave the room, and later she wrote home:

> I knew they had Bibles out and that Fran was progressing towards asking Dr Otten for a decision . . . I prayed fervently that this might be the night of salvation for dear Doctor Otten. I had a strange experience, because as the voices were low, I could not know what was being said, and during my fervent and earnest pleading with the Lord, I suddenly was filled with a peace—and even as I attempted to continue my praying—my mind was filled with the phrase, 'It is finished.' I became convinced that the Lord had answered and the need for that particular prayer was finished.[1]

Fran later reported that Dr Otten had given his life to Christ.

We might ask why the Holy Spirit sometimes takes so long to answer our prayers. Why did God take so long to apply the truth persuasively to Dr Otten? Could it be that God wanted a deep and personal relationship of mutual love and respect to be built between Dr Otten and the Schaeffers? God knew only much time and many prayers would forge that association into a thing of lasting value. In praying for others, we often need to look beyond the immediate concern to learn why God will sometimes take longer than we expect to answer our prayers.

As we think of why we must often pray a long time for some things, we need to remember that receiving speedy answers all the time can make us arrogant and fill us with pride. We can come to believe that God's answers are our accomplishments, that the conversion of sinners is our work, that our faith is the basic reason for God's answers instead of His love for us and others. We can come to think more highly of ourselves than we ought. When God moved and Dr Otten was converted, the Schaeffers praised God instead of complimenting themselves.

The time that Fran and Edith spent praying for Dr Otten and preparing his lessons drew their hearts closer to him. He could sense their sincere love for him and saw their concern for his salvation. He was not just another number to be

won to the Lord, but a real person whose eternal
salvation meant much to them. Their prayers
enabled him to sense the personal love and
concern of Jesus Christ *for him through them*. Much
prayer for sinners brings about a bond of unity and
love that nothing else will.

If God had answered their prayers quickly,
Fran might never have finished the many Bible
lessons he wrote for just one person. Eventually,
Edith typed these lessons over and over again for
others, and God has used them to lead countless
numbers to saving faith.[2] Hence, we learn that
God's delay will often bring blessings far beyond
the original intention of our prayers. Many have
been blessed because Dr Otten waited until 1952 to
commit his life to Jesus Christ.

When God is slow in answering our prayers,
we need to keep on praying until we receive a yes
or no answer. When God is slow in answering our
prayers, we need to ask Him if He wants us to do
more than pray. God inspired Fran to write his
Bible lessons for Dr Otten, and then led him to read
them. When God is slow in answering our
prayers, we can pray that more people will be
blessed through His delay than if He had answered
quickly. It may be that God wants to spread the
gospel net wider and wider as we pray, and that
He is slow only as we count slowness.

Sometimes God will reveal to us directly by

97

His Spirit that our prayers have been answered, and then we trust in faith that He has heard. But Edith did not stop praying until the Holy Spirit gave her the sense, 'It is finished.' If we stop praying too soon, God may choose not to complete the work we have been praying to see accomplished. Some work in us and others He will accomplish only *through much prayer*. If God removes our burden to pray for someone and gives us peace, we need to praise Him for this special revelation as well as the answer. Edith did not seek the experience God gave her regarding Dr Otten's conversion. He spoke to her in an unusual way that would strengthen her faith and teach her more about the power of prayer in the conversion of sinners.

As we pray, God will sometimes give us strong feelings for someone's salvation. As we pray for them, we will draw nearer to God and to the person God has placed on our hearts. When the person is converted, we will rejoice in God for what He has done. These experiences in prayer flow naturally from the benevolent concern for others God has placed in our hearts. Satan cannot counterfeit these benevolent, spiritual experiences, for he is the bringer of death, not the giver of life.

Prayer

Dear Heavenly Father, encourage me when I am tempted to give up and not pray for others—especially for their salvation. Show me anything more that I may need to do besides pray, and then give me the courage and wisdom to do it. Show me the abundance of blessings that can flow from my prayers, so I will pray more and more and praise You for hearing my feeble words. In the power of the Holy Spirit, help me to bless as many people as I can by everything I do. From time to time, please encourage me by showing me some of the effects through history of the work I do in Your Way and Spirit. In Jesus' name. Amen.

─── 11 ───────

GOD GIVES MORE THAN WE ASK

> *Now to him who is able to do immeasurably more than all we ask or imagine, according to his power that is at work within us, to him be glory in the church and in Christ Jesus throughout all generations, for ever and ever! Amen.*
>
> **Ephesians 3:20–21**

Francis Schaeffer emphasised that Jesus Christ reigned as Lord over the whole of life. And when he began to write and publish his books in the 1960s, he demonstrated this truth and inspired people to work for the extension of God's Kingdom over every area of life. For Fran, believing Jesus is Lord was not just a theological statement of faith. He desired to live totally under the lordship of Christ; therefore, God answered his prayers and met the daily needs of his family. Fran learned from the Bible and experience that Jesus ruled over all, and this gave his message an urgency that led many to follow the Saviour.

In Switzerland, Fran and Edith had to work out the details for their children's education, so that they would be prepared to attend either an American or a European university. When they prayed, schools were found. If the school became inappropriate, they prayed again, and God provided another school and even the money for them to attend. Their Heavenly Father was just as concerned about preparing their children for their future work as they were. Because God wanted their children to learn subjects in a variety of different fields, and not be confined to just the 'spiritual things' and a knowledge of the Bible, they can do many things and are highly effective witnesses to all types of people.

One day Priscilla told her parents that she needed help in Algebra. They asked her to pray about it, thinking that God would give her the understanding she needed. And they all prayed for her that evening. The next day, a mathematics professor from a nearby school and his wife called on the Schaeffers at their home. They had some deep theological questions brought on from false teachings, and one Sunday at church they had sensed that Fran might have the answers they needed. They came to spend the afternoon so Fran could clear up their confusions. Fran answered question after question until 2:00 a.m., when Professor Czerny and his wife bowed their heads and received Jesus Christ as their Lord and Saviour with an understanding of what that meant.

As we have seen, God can use us and our prayers for years to lead someone to salvation, or He can take only a few hours or minutes. The mystery of God's work in salvation remains with Him, but whether quickly or not, God has wise and loving reasons for His perfect timing in answers to prayer.

Priscilla had served as the translator throughout Fran's discussions with Professor Czerny and his wife, and in appreciation for Fran's teaching they asked if they could do anything for them. With amazed looks at one another, they exclaimed that Priscilla needed a tutor in Algebra, and Mr Czerny readily agreed to help her. Later,

Professor Czerny met Mr Exhenry, and they became the first two elders in the International Presbyterian Church.

God prepared the Schaeffers for the eventual founding of L'Abri and for demonstrating His existence through answered prayer by responding to their prayers in every area of life and by meeting their every practical need. They saw God working every day of their lives. Fran and Edith did not reserve prayer for only the spiritual things, or the big things, or the major problems, or the conversion of sinners. They tried to maintain an open and constant communication with the Lord throughout the day—seeking His will and taking everything to God in prayer. Because they knew God was their Heavenly Father, they knew He was concerned about every aspect of their lives and their whole family.

When they prayed for Priscilla to have help in maths, God taught them that He could provide a tutor as easily as give her the understanding she needed without one. He taught them something about His economy: the Schaeffers could share their knowledge of salvation with a professor who could then share his knowledge of maths with them. And God gave Priscilla a born-again teacher who, as a new believer, would learn as much about the things of the Lord from her as she would learn about maths from him. God gave everyone immeasurably more than they asked or thought when they prayed.

When God begins to teach us more about prayer, He will sometimes allow us to have an unusual need that He will meet in a special way only in answer to our prayers. And then He will wait until we have prayed. And He will not answer us until He is certain that the time is right and we will learn the lesson that He intends for us. God uses many different ways to teach us about His loving nature and longing to hear us pray, and then He cares for us in all things.

The Schaeffers did not always receive a visible answer to their prayers the very next day. As we have seen, they only received some answers after months of persevering prayer, because God must prepare us and others to receive the answer in the way that will do the most good and build up people's faith in the process. Far more is involved in God's answers to prayer than we will ever understand in this life. Not receiving an immediate answer does not necessarily mean that we are spiritually out of touch with God or being punished for some sin. It may simply mean that God has many lessons to teach us and others before giving us the answers we seek.

Some answers to prayer come like the building of a house. The land must be surveyed and bought, and the plans must be drawn and the

foundation laid in just the right order. The frame is
constructed before the walls are built and the roof
is added. When God answers prayers, He does so
with order and precision. And sometimes He will
teach us to pray in the right order for things before
He will answer our prayers, or He will answer a
series of prayers one at a time as we learn to pray
for each new need or step. God wants us to learn
to think logically, and use our mind as well as our
spirit in prayer. As Paul wrote, 'So what shall I do?
I will pray with my spirit, but I will also pray with
my mind; I will sing with my spirit, but I will also
sing with my mind' (1 Corinthians 14:15). When
God answers our prayers in the right order, He
reveals something about His nature and character,
and meets the needs of our logical minds. Through
prayer, God will strengthen and discipline our
rational ways of thinking. And then we will praise
Him more and more for building our faith in Him
with every answer He gives to every request.

If the Schaeffers had not prayed for Priscilla to
get help in mathematics, the professor might never
have knocked on their door, or they might never
have seen his coming as a specific answer to their
prayers. Over the years, the Schaeffers came to
believe that every person who knocked on their
door was sent in answer to prayer, theirs or
someone else's, and was special. If the Schaeffers
had put their needs before the professor's and

asked for his help immediately, the professor and his wife might never have had the time they needed to come to the Lord quickly. Having learned the lesson of praying for God's timing and words from an unselfish heart, God could send them just the right help when needed.

Prayer

Dear Father, teach me the lessons about prayer that You want me to learn from this book, so You will not need to spend years teaching me what You can teach me now. For Jesus' sake. Amen.

12

THE BATTLE IN PRAYER AND SATAN

And pray that we may be delivered from wicked and evil men, for not everyone has faith.

2 Thessalonians 3:2

Since Francis and Edith Schaeffer walked with God throughout the day and tried to maintain a life of prayer and purity in the Lord Jesus Christ, God sometimes forewarned them about a difficult period ahead and moved them to send out an urgent call for prayer. We see this particularly in Edith's letters home. On 10 January, 1953, she asked for prayer and said, 'When the Holy Spirit is working, the devil is sure to attempt to hinder and your prayers are needed.'[1] After almost five years of unprecedented answers to prayer and success in witnessing with little opposition, Satan began to take special notice of what the Schaeffers were doing in their small corner of the world. The devil's attacks and various afflictions seemed to engulf them, beginning in 1953, and continued to plague them through the early years of L'Abri. But God used every one of their trials and tribulations to teach them more about prayer and show them His power to deliver.

Over the succeeding years as God answered their prayers, He often did so in the context of overcoming afflictions and defeating Satan. In her letters, Edith's prayer requests of others became almost the continual call 'that Satan be defeated or disappointed'. In 1953, God began to show them more and more about the spiritual battle ahead, and that Satan could use the government, non-believers, and even other Christians to attack them and His work. God did this to show the new people who needed to be saved or who studied at L'Abri that He could defeat Satan or give a believer the grace to persevere in trouble in answer to the fervent and persistent prayers of themselves and others.[2] These facts about the power of prayer in affliction needed to be demonstrated time and time again to different people, and this meant real suffering.

Before they left for their furlough in America, after five years in Switzerland, Fran faced a spiritual crisis, an attack upon his faith and God's faithfulness, a loss of the reality of walking with God in His way, a dark cloud that Satan lowered. Paul might have described such an experience with these words: 'For the flesh sets its desire against the Spirit, and the Spirit against the flesh; for these are in opposition to one another, so that you may not do the things that you please. But if you are led by the Spirit, you are not under the Law' (Galatians 5:17–18 NASB). Or perhaps Peter better described Fran's problem when he warned, 'Be self-controlled and alert. Your enemy the devil prowls around like a roaring lion looking for someone to devour' (1 Peter 5:8).

Fran walked and prayed in the hayloft of Chalet Bijou in poor weather and in the mountains whenever possible. He thought through everything once again from his early scepticism to the present, and God renewed his faith, love and joy. The Holy Spirit guided him as Satan tried to destroy what God had been building in Fran's soul. And God won an even greater victory through Fran's testing by giving him an experience

111

and knowledge that allowed him to write a series of lectures on sanctification that he taught many times while on furlough in America.[3]

Unfortunately, some of the leaders in his denomination did not appreciate Fran's lectures and call to show forth God's love as they fought for the truth. The conflict became so heated, that in the middle of their seventeen-month furlough the Lord showed the Schaeffers that they would need to pray for the funds to return to Switzerland. They decided not to write letters describing their plight and requesting money, but take their need to the Lord alone in prayer. The girls made a thermometer, and coloured it in as they received funds for their boat fare. They needed their ticket money by 29 July, 1954 to make reservations, but it came in so slowly they had to remind the girls that God might be showing them that His will was for them to remain in America rather than return to Switzerland, and all they wanted was God's will for their lives. From unexpected sources, once again God met their needs right before the 29th, and the Schaeffers sent for their tickets home.

Through their prayers for boat passage, God reminded the Schaeffers that He would often providentially use money, its lack or provision, to show them His will. By His Spirit and through circumstances, He gave them enough warning to begin praying soon enough for Him to work and give them the answer in a way that would do them the most good spiritually. Rather than wait until the last minute, in the middle of their furlough they began praying for money. God could have answered their last-minute prayers and sometimes did; however, this time God inspired them to begin praying immediately.

God often prefers to show us the need for persistent prayer to build up our relationship with Him and increase our faith when He gives the answer. Through much prayer, God and His will often become more important than the answer we want, and God wants us to be in that state of heart. After eight months of prayer and patient waiting, the money for their boat passage came the day it was needed. What a wonderful way for God to inspire real rejoicing for His answers to prayer!

God will often delay an answer so that we will pray fervently for something to show ourselves and Him just how much we want the answer. In His great mercy, God will sometimes delay an answer until we discover that the very thing we are praying for we really do not want or need, or do not want seriously enough to persist in prayer until we get the answer. Through much prayer, each member of the Schaeffer family discovered that they earnestly desired to continue the work God had begun through them in Switzerland, and no attacks from Satan or the people who misunderstood them would deter them from doing what they believed God wanted them to do. God gave them this deep desire to continue their work and met their need, so once they returned their increasing difficulties would not overwhelm them.

God often shows us His will and how to pray from the providential things that are happening around us. While they were in America, God reminded the Schaeffers that He could be trusted more than people, but that He could use people to meet their needs by prayer alone. God taught them this valuable lesson, so that they would have the courage to step out in faith when it was time to begin L'Abri and trust in God alone.

In the battle against Satan and in our search for God's will, we must observe all that is taking place around us, because God will use history, the lives of others, the state of the church and our situation to reveal His will providentially to us. When we understand God's will from providence, we need to pray that His will may be accomplished.

Prayer

Dear Heavenly Father, help me prevail as I battle in prayer. Help me discover whether the opposition I face is from Satan or from Your desire to direct me in a different way. Show me Your will as I draw close to You, and keep me from deception. Keep me from blaming Satan for anything sinful in my thoughts, desires or way of life that may be delaying your answers to prayer. Help me turn from all unrighteousness so that my prayers will be effective in defeating all of Satan's schemes. By Your Spirit, show me Your will in the events taking place all around me, so I will know how to pray according to Your will and real needs. Amen.

13

THE BATTLE IN PRAYER AND THE BIBLE

In the first year of his reign, I, Daniel, understood from the Scriptures, according to the word of the LORD given to Jeremiah the prophet, that the desolation of Jerusalem would last seventy years. So I turned to the Lord God and pleaded with him in prayer and petition, in fasting, and in sackcloth and ashes.

Daniel 9:2–3

*O*n the Schaeffers' way back to Europe, their two-year-old son, Franky, had a polio attack. While Edith was in the hospital praying about his experimental treatments, the Lord reminded her that she could apply the Bible's general promises to specific situations in prayer. As she prayed, the Holy Spirit prompted her to pray according to Proverbs 21:1—'The king's heart is in the hand of the LORD; he directs it like a watercourse wherever he pleases.' The Holy Spirit told her that she should pray for the doctor in the context of this verse. God could make a doctor's decisions as easily as He could a king's. And it did not matter whether the doctor or the king were believers or unbelievers. In the Old Testament, God often accomplished great things through pagan rulers— with no credit to them and often without their knowledge—and He does the same today. At the last minute, when the doctor came and looked at Franky, he decided not to do the treatment. This answer describes how God teaches us to pray in the context of His predictions and promises in the Bible.

We need to pray for God's will to be done in the context of the Bible's predictions and promises just as much as Daniel prayed for Jeremiah's prophecy to be fulfilled after the seventy-year captivity was completed. God uses the Bible to teach us the things He wants us to pray about. And in Daniel's case, as he read the Old Testament that was still being formed, the Holy Spirit pointed out that God had completed Judah's punishment as foretold by Jeremiah. So Daniel prayed, pleaded, and fasted in deep humility for God to work upon their captives' minds and wills to free His people. Daniel also prayed that God would use him in the leadership position in which He had placed him, and show him what to do to fulfil God's prophetic Word. Daniel saw his place of authority in the kingdom as a part of God's providential care in that specific time to free His people. So Daniel sought the Lord's guidance and was willing to accept any responsibility that God wanted him to fulfil.

If we ask God to reveal His biblical promises to us while showing us His providential work taking place around us, He will give us great encouragement in prayer and we will receive God's guidance on how to pray. We can pray and plead for God to complete His work in the context of His promises and predictions, believing that He is always faithful to keep His word. By enlightening our minds through His written Word and visible work in our midst, God increases our faith, encourages us to pray, and deepens our fellowship with Him.

As we read the Bible, praying for God to

speak to us through His Word, sometimes He makes a verse, promise or prediction stand out on the page as though it were highlighted or underlined to guide us in our prayers. We may read a verse, parable or historical incident, and the Holy Spirit may speak to our hearts something like: 'This Word is for you personally. This Word is my reply to your concern. This verse shows you what to pray and do. Keep on praying. If you want Me to fill this need, you will need to fast. Fasting will draw us closer and enable you to hear me more clearly.' Edith's Bible is a diary of dated prayers in the context of the verses she has read.

God expects us to fill our minds with His Word and read the Bible daily so that He can speak to us each day. As we pray, sometimes God will remind us of a verse from the Bible that we read long ago. The verse will come into our minds completely unexpectedly, so that we will know that the Holy Spirit has given us that verse to encourage us to pray and expect an answer according to that particular promise of God.

In Edith's case, the Holy Spirit reminded her directly of a verse that she had learned many years before so that she could apply a prayer principle. God told her to pray for Franky's treatment in the context of that verse describing how God can work upon all people in places of responsibility. We too can use that verse as we pray in similar situations.

We must make an effort to receive God's teaching on prayer. If we are unwilling to spend the time or make the effort to read God's Word with the attitude that we will obey whatever understanding He gives us as we read, then the times when God speaks to us in the context of His Word as we pray will be rare.

When Satan tempted Jesus to sin in the wilderness, Jesus replied correctly with the Scriptures, because Jesus knew the Old Testament. Because He prayed long and often, He recognised the Holy Spirit's help in applying God's Word rightly in that situation. When Satan tried to twist God's Word, Jesus knew the context of the Scriptures so well that with the Holy Spirit's help He defeated the devil at every point. Jesus prepared Himself for thirty years, committed Himself publicly to serving God when John baptised Him, and allowed Himself to be led by the Holy Spirit into the wilderness to defeat the devil. Jesus' wholehearted commitment and preparation enabled Him to turn back Satan's attack and receive the ministrations of God's angels after Satan fled from His presence (see Matthew 3 and 4).

If God required Daniel to pray in the context of His Word, and if God required Jesus to pray, study His Word, and prepare Himself to serve Him, we tempt God if we think we can do less and receive God's blessings in their fullness. God will always be gracious to His children, but we open the door for God to do so much more when we decide to follow Jesus, no matter what the cost in time or hard thinking in a thorough study of His Word.

God loves us so much that He will sometimes bless us in unexpected ways even though we have not learned much about prayer or His promises in the Bible. God often helps us because He loves us and wants to meet our needs. However, we need to seek Him more *for who He is*, and learn the principles He has established for prevailing prayer so that we can bless others as well as ourselves through prayer.

God gave us His Word to read, think about, and use in the context of prayer, and if we are not growing spiritually the reason may be our failure to use all the means of grace that God has provided. A disruptive, inattentive student in a classroom will learn a few things, but the dedicated, hardworking student will be prepared for life. We cannot expect to learn the deep things of God and all that He has for us if we are like disruptive and inattentive students throughout the day. Disciplining ourselves with set times for Bible reading and prayer, beginning each day in God's Word, developing the habit of putting God and His will first, and looking to see His visible work each day will help us overcome the bad habits of poor or new students in God's school of prayer.

Prayer

Dear Father, fill me with Your love and help me love You so much that I will long to spend time with You. Show me the importance of much prayer and Bible study. Keep me from being selfish and self-centred, so that these things will not be a burden to me but the desire of my heart. Help me to recognise Your work around me, in my home, church, neighbourhood and world, so that I can pray specifically and not just in generalities. Truly You are worthy to receive all glory and honour. In Jesus' name. Amen.

14

PRAYING THROUGH THE PROMISES OF GOD

> *In the last days the mountain of the LORD's temple will be established as chief among the mountains; it will be raised above the hills, and all nations will stream to it. Many peoples will come and say, 'Come, let us go up to the mountain of the LORD, to the house of the God of Jacob. He will teach us his ways, so that we may walk in his paths.' The law will go out from Zion, the word of the LORD from Jerusalem.*

Isaiah 2:2–3

As 1954 drew to a close, the Schaeffers celebrated the founding of their International Church; however, after their furlough, they had few reasons to rejoice. Right after learning Franky had polio, they discovered Susan had rheumatic fever. As they coped with these attacks on their health, Fran received some complaint letters from his mission board and the notice that their salary was being reduced by $100 per month. When we remember that in 1954 a nice, spacious chalet could be bought for less than $20,000, the cut was devastating.

As they prayed for the Lord's leading about whether they should begin L'Abri as a work of faith and about what to do next (since they believed the Lord returned them to Switzerland for a purpose), they learned that opposition to their remaining in Champéry was being raised by some villagers because of Mr Exhenry's new-found faith. Then they learned their permit to stay in Switzerland might be revoked, because of their religious influence in the village. They wondered if they would have to leave their chalet and work. And then as they prayed in the light of these new uncertainties, they were almost killed when their chalet was nearly swept away by avalanches.[1]

As Satan attacked them from without, literally using misguided believers, nonbelievers, their neighbours, nature, their health, the government and everything that he could throw against them, he also began to attack them spiritually by tempting them to distrust God and disbelieve in His providential care for them. We can imagine Satan taunting them: 'Did God *really* lead you back here? Does God *really* want you to stay. Shouldn't you pack up and go home? God is not faithful, is He?'

But as the devil attacked them fiercely, tempting them to deny God's faithfulness, God expressed His love for them more vividly. The Holy Spirit drew them closer to God, and they leaned more upon Jesus Christ and read their Bible more. They bowed before Jesus in submission and rededication once again, and vowed they would follow His leading no matter what the cost. The Holy Spirit used the Word of God and their prayers to teach them new lessons, and as they learned these lessons things began to change. Many and newer afflictions continued, but God also answered their prayers in the midst of all of these, and strengthened their faith and witness. Those who had become Christians through their testimony saw them demonstrate their faith in God and love for others in the good times as well as the bad, and the devil lost his battle to lead others astray.

And then, in January of 1955, the Holy Spirit gave Edith a wonderful new promise from the

Bible. As her reading progressed through the Old Testament, the Holy Spirit wrote the words of Isaiah, chapter 2, verses 2 and 3 on her heart and mind as a personal promise to her. Yes, Isaiah had specifically foretold events to take place in Judaea, but the Holy Spirit told Edith that God was going to do something very similar in the Swiss Alps through them. Edith shared this promise with the family, and as they prayed they claimed this specific promise as a reality for the new work that God would begin as He continued what He had begun in their lives. They prayed, and almost forty years later we know with certainty that God kept His promise and answered the prayers He inspired them to make according to His Word.

When a situation changes and we are kept from doing what we intended or what we thought God had wanted us to do, we need to pray for God to show us something else we can do in the new situation. Satan will be defeated over and over again, even as situations change, when we are faithful to seek only God's will, pray for the strength to do it, and then follow God no matter what the personal cost or sacrifice. For example, when the Romans chained Paul and cast him into prison, so he could not preach any longer in the market place, he praised God, sang hymns, preached to the guards and other prisoners, and wrote letters that changed lives. Through prayer, total dedication to Jesus Christ, and a willingness to die if need be, God will show us how to serve Him in every situation. If a guard hired to defend the queen has committed himself to the possibility of casting himself before her to stop the assassin's bullet, should we refuse to do any less for the Sovereign King of the universe? Our total commitment to God will be tested in a variety of ways, but each way gives us the opportunity to re-examine our lives, recommit ourselves, and learn new lessons in the school of obedient prayer.

Because the Schaeffers spent much time in prayer and regular reading of the Bible, they opened their minds to being taught directly by the Holy Spirit as they studied God's Word. God gave them Scripture verses from time to time that spoke directly to their prayer concerns. And then the Holy Spirit motivated them to ask God to fulfil the promises in His Word. Many times the Holy Spirit would use this method to demonstrate God's power and loving faithfulness. They prayed fervently and worked hard to build just what the Lord foretold He would do through them. They did not sit back and wait and watch, without praying for God to show them what they could do *that* day towards the accomplishment of His will in the strength *He* would give for *that* day alone.

God gives general and specific promises in the Bible to build our faith in Him as we pray. These promises become the evidence for a reasonable faith that God will do what He has promised. For example, Jesus promised believers, 'For if you forgive men when they sin against you, your heavenly Father will also forgive you' and 'Ask and it will be given to you; seek and you will find; knock and the door will be opened to you. For everyone who asks receives; he who seeks finds; and to him who knocks, the door will be opened' (Matthew 6:14; 7:7–8).

When we pray, we can trust God to fulfil these promises. All we need to do is fulfil the conditions that He has set forth as we pray. As He said, when we forgive we have the assurance of God's forgiveness according to His promise (see also 1 John 1:9). As the Bible teaches, we need to comply with God's commands and ask in order to receive according to His promises. If we are asking and not receiving, then we may be violating some other principle. For example, we may be asking with selfish motives (James 4:3). Or, God may be answering the spirit of our prayer.

As we live and pray on the basis of the Bible's general promises, God will sometimes give us a specific promise and confirm it by the Holy Spirit or providence. This was the case with the Isaiah passage for the Schaeffers and L'Abri. They prayed and worked to fulfil every condition God revealed in His Word, so that His work would be established in the mountains, and eventually their work became a worldwide ministry.

Prayer

Dear Father, show me the promises that I should learn from the Bible. Enlighten my mind and apply them by Your Spirit. Keep me from vain delusions. Keep me from following impulses and feelings. Lead me by Your revealed Word and works. Amen.

MY FATHER'S HOUSE

And as he taught them, he said, 'Is it not written: "My house will be called a house of prayer for all nations"? But you have made it "a den of robbers".'

Mark 11:17

God sometimes forewarns us to encourage us and help us through the dark times ahead, but we may or may not be sensitive enough to hear Him. Before their many trials began to bury them in the Alps, God granted Edith a premonition into the future and revealed the purpose for tribulations. She almost prophetically wrote home from their boat on 3 September, 1954:

> Our ways are not the Lord's ways, and how can we experience His sufficiency in all things, His comfort in tribulation, if we never go through the times of tribulation? We need to experience all kinds of tribulation if we are also to experience His wonderful ways of bringing us through and supplying our every need.[1]

Apparently, they *needed* to experience all the tribulations they suffered in the founding and early years of L'Abri, and that is why Edith sometimes asks people who say they would like to have a life like hers, 'Are you willing to pay the price of hardship and suffering?'

In their afflictions, God demonstrated His love and provision time and time again. If He did not remove the affliction, He sustained them through it and increased their faith and joy. And after showing them the sufficiency of His grace, *then* He often removed the affliction. God also used their afflictions, their faith, and His answers to prayers in times of trouble to lead many nonbelievers to a saving faith in Jesus Christ. They saw God's mighty power at work and defeating

Satan's schemes, so that they came to believe in God and turn to Him in prayer. Satan sifted the Schaeffers just as he tested Job, and we can see today that he did not prevail over them any more than he defeated Job.

Through training and tribulation, God made the Schaeffers' home and L'Abri into a House of Prayer. Jesus said, 'My house will be called a house of prayer for all nations,' and, by beginning in one small chalet tucked away in Switzerland, that is exactly what God made L'Abri. Thousands of people from almost every nation and religion would eventually come to L'Abri, find God and learn how to talk with Him. Through the Schaeffers' work, God intended to teach all believers that they needed to look upon their homes as 'Houses of Prayer', rather than thinking only of the Temple in Jerusalem or their own church as places of intercession. Through L'Abri, God would show the Church what she needed to become to be *His* house—she needed to be a House of Prayer. God never intended the Church or our homes to be a place of withdrawal from responsibility for the state of the world, but a place to intercede for the material and spiritual needs of others, a place to do spiritual battle for the souls of men, women and children. A House of Prayer is not a place for withdrawing into our minds or spirits to experience 'something spiritual' or to take a 'spiritual trip', but a place where everything is taken to the Lord in prayer and time is spent simply talking to our Heavenly Father, as we would to any other person we have come to love, enjoy being with, and respect.

However, if God wanted the Schaeffer home to be a House of Prayer, He would need to provide the house and maintain it, for on 14 February, 1955, Swiss authorities gave the Schaeffers until 31 March to leave Swiss soil. This blow almost devastated them, especially when they thought of all the work it had taken to build up their overseas ministry and how difficult it would be to start life over again completely. As they thought about the possible alternatives, Edith reminded them of the Lord's promise to her from Isaiah. As they learned more about the edict of eviction, it seemed they could stay in Switzerland *if* they could find a new home in a canton that would accept them. They prayed, asked everyone who supported their work to pray, talked to the authorities, and began to look for a new home they could afford.

They could not afford any house they were shown, until Edith found Chalet les Mélèzes in Huemoz. The day she saw it, Edith prayed for a sign from the Lord, that if He wanted them to buy the house He would send them $1,000 *the very next day* in the mail. She had never been so bold and asked for something that seemed impossible

before, but she prayed and believed that with God
all things are possible. The next day, before she left
with Fran on the train to show him the chalet, they
received their mail—and found a cheque for
$1,000. Some dear friends in Ohio had written in
their letter that 'The Lord, they felt, had led them
to send it to the Schaeffers to start a fund to buy a
house where young people would come to learn
more about the Lord Jesus.'[2] The Holy Spirit had
provided His answer even before He had inspired
her to go boldly to the Lord with an 'impossible'
request.[3] This three-storey chalet, completely
furnished, would cost them about $17,000, but they
had to trust in the Lord's leading for the rest of the
money to be given *in time* to make the necessary
payments. When the first payment was due, they
counted their gifts in their 'house' fund, and
discovered that they had $3.52 more than they
needed. For most of the time in L'Abri, and even
to this day, God works just this closely to provide
their needs—one day at a time.

While these attacks on the Schaeffers were
taking place, their two new elders in the
International Church were suffering too. Professor
and Mrs Czerny's son died, and Mr Exhenry's
wife, who was Roman Catholic, threatened to
separate from him. So as the Schaeffers and those
who loved them prayed for the Schaeffers' needs,
they also prayed for their church leaders and

members, because the devil was trying to destroy all that God was building through them. However, the more Satan fought, the more God opened some people's eyes, and when the children's piano teacher learned about their afflictions and subsequent eviction, and saw their steadfast faith and love for God even in adversities, she believed in the Lord Jesus Christ for salvation. And their new elders remained faithful and steadfast in their witnessing to others in the midst of their troubles.

In the fires of affliction, God brought them a greater revival and reformation, and Edith wrote home:

> We ask only that we may be filled with the Spirit so that His plan may in no wise be hindered by our flesh . . . He does *time* things perfectly, and we need to keep our minds stayed on Him so that we will not be 'anxious' in anything—but truly bring to Him the needs both material and spiritual with *thanksgiving*.[4]

In their tribulations, God gave the Schaeffers the opportunity to practise their biblical faith in the power of the Holy Spirit, and this consistency in the dark times led some to believe who would otherwise never have seen God's sufficient grace in all situations.

Prayer

Dear Father, in the difficult days, remind me that spiritual victories do not come cheaply. Give me that inner peace that passes all understanding, and keep me from running away from the battles You want me to fight using the spiritual means You have provided. Help me to bring everything to You in prayer, by quietly drawing me by Your Spirit to tell You everything and intercede for all who have needs. As I study the spiritual biographies of others, encourage me and teach me to learn the spiritual principles You want me to apply in my life, and keep me from copying someone's life for the wrong reasons. Help me do all that You want me to do to glorify You and Your Son. Amen.

— 16 ——————

MY FATHER'S PLANS

> *'For I know the plans I have for you,' declares the*
> *LORD, 'plans to prosper you and not to harm you,*
> *plans to give you hope and a future. Then you*
> *will call upon me and come and pray to me, and I*
> *will listen to you. You will seek me and find me*
> *when you seek me with all your heart.'*
>
> **Jeremiah 29:11–13**

*F*ran often said that we need to see things in the
context of the Bible and the whole of Christian
history, not just in the light of our own lives and

personal experiences. L'Abri did not begin just in the context of the Schaeffers' own experiences, but with the additional confirmation of how God had worked in those they read about in the Bible and history. The prayer principles they used to start L'Abri were not new to them. They had been tried and tested by people like Hudson Taylor and George Müller, and the Schaeffers had proved their reliability over the years.

True faith must be based on evidence, evidence that God has given in the Bible and through His active work in creation and history. Paul discussed such evidence in his letter to the Romans: 'For since the creation of the world God's invisible qualities—his eternal power and divine nature—have been clearly seen, being understood from what has been made, so that men are without excuse'(Romans 1:20). In addition to this evidence, the Schaeffers believed that God gave evidence of His existence through their work, and that all evidence of His existence can be passed on to others to lead them to faith or strengthen their beliefs. Faith did not involve a leap of faith contrary to good and sufficient reasons to believe in God. True faith involves understanding and accepting the Bible as the Word of God, and choosing to live one's life on the basis of God's Word. True faith includes bowing before Jesus Christ and accepting Him as Lord, the second

Person in the Trinity, and our Saviour from sin and hell. True faith consists of choosing to follow the day-to-day leading of the Holy Spirit and seeking to be filled with Him so we will follow the Spirit and not the flesh. True faith leads to purity of life and a concern for leading others to the Saviour.

When the Schaeffers began L'Abri, all of these elements of faith were involved in their decision. *Not* to have begun L'Abri when they did would have meant disobeying God, for God had given them good and sufficient reasons that this was His will for their lives—plans for a hope and future, to prosper them so that they could help others.

To pray with faith that we are praying according to the will of God demands evidence that what we are praying for is indeed according to His will. Praying with faith means that we have chosen to accept the good and sufficient evidence God has given that He wants us to pray for particular blessings, and then praying for the specific things God has shown us until we have received them. As Jeremiah wrote, once we understand that God has plans for us, we should pray for God to reveal His plans. And when we begin to understand His plans, we can come to Him in faith and pray on the basis of His promise to listen to our prayers. As we seek and find God, we can praise Him and thank Him for His leading and tender mercies, for His gift of life and hope, for

His gift of service to others according to His power which works within us.

The Schaeffers began L'Abri and began praying for its success *after* God had given them evidence of His will using the four means He will use to give us faith in prayer—the faith that we are praying according to His will. Sometimes God will give us faith to pray for something specific by using only one of these means, but when He uses all four means we can pray with boldness and thanksgiving that God will achieve His purposes through our prayers. As we have seen, over the years, God taught the Schaeffers to recognise and follow His use of these means to reveal His will for how they should pray: the *Holy Spirit*, the general and specific *promises in the Bible*, *predictions in the Bible*, and *providential events* in their lives and world.

As we read the Bible through each day, not skipping from place to place thinking we will discover God's plan by opening the Bible at random places looking for His 'magic' Word to us, we need to pray believing and asking for the Holy Spirit to show us any commands or promises God has for us that we need to follow. In Jeremiah, chapter 29, we find a general promise that any believer can use when he prays. In the verses above, God has given us the evidence we need to believe that *if we seek Him with all our heart*, we will

144

find Him and He will unfold for us His plan for
our lives. He may not show us everything at once,
but He will lead us daily to fulfil His plan if we
will pray, seek His will and choose to follow Him
in the Holy Spirit's power.

As we read through the Bible, we also need to
pray for the Holy Spirit to show us any predictions
that we might apply to our lives. Usually, the Holy
Spirit will not show these to us until we have first
learned how to obey God and apply and obey the
Bible's promises. Edith did not receive the Holy
Spirit's inspiration and motivation to accept the
prediction from Isaiah 2:2–3 for them until after she
had learned a lot about God and prayer from His
promises. If she had not spent much time in Bible
study and prayer over the years, she would not
have recognised these verses as God speaking
directly to them. The Holy Spirit built upon all
that God had taught her through a life of prayer, so
she would accept this passage as evidence for the
faith she needed to pray that God would build
L'Abri through them in the mountains.

As we look around us, we need to ask the
Holy Spirit to show us any special work that God
is doing in our midst, that we are to recognise as a
special work of providence for guidance in
prayer—so we can pray in faith that God wants to
give us the blessing. When Edith saw Chalet les
Mélèzes in Huemoz for the first time, the Holy

Spirit led her to pray for this home through the providence of her finding it and its being perfect for L'Abri in so many ways, and then the Holy Spirit prompted her to pray for a specific amount of money to confirm His leading.

As we pray, sometimes the Holy Spirit will speak to our spirits directly. As Edith prayed for God to make their living in Chalet les Mélèzes possible, she first began to pray that the owner would change his mind and rent it instead of insisting that it be sold. However, the Holy Spirit stopped her and moved her to pray specifically for the money to buy it, and set a deadline and amount for a confirmation of God's will. Because she knew the Spirit's voice, she prayed for $1,000. And the Holy Spirit filled the family with joy when $1,000 was sent with perfect timing. Through the gift's arrival in the next day's mail, God assured the Schaeffers that they were moving according to His plan.

Living by faith and prayer demands that we spend quality time with God by reading His Word and praying. Time spent in prayer will not substitute for time spent reading the Bible, and time spent reading the Bible will not take the place of getting to know God better through conversational prayer. As we demonstrate our dedication to God and open up our hearts to His leading, He will speak to us more and more through the Holy

Spirit, the Bible's promises and predictions, and through providential events. Only by spending time with God, and by learning about His character and ways of working in the Bible, will God build our faith on solid evidence so that we can avoid the pitfalls of following our feelings, impulses or selfish desires, as though these were the Spirit's leading. To avoid following the wrong spirits and people, we need to know God and His Word so well that we will not be deceived.

Prayer

Dear Father, thank You for the safeguards You have given, so we will not be misled or pray in the wrong spirit for the wrong things. Increase my faith so I can pray rightly. Amen.

— 17 —

MY FATHER'S PROVISIONS

And foreigners who bind themselves to the LORD
to serve him, to love the name of the LORD, *and to
worship him, all who keep the Sabbath without
desecrating it and who hold fast to my
covenant—these I will bring to my holy mountain
and give them joy in my house of prayer. Their
burnt offerings and sacrifices will be accepted on
my altar; for my house will be called a house of
prayer for all nations.*

Isaiah 56:6–7

*I*n 1955, when the Schaeffers received notice to leave Switzerland by the end of March, they experienced the feelings of refugees and unwanted foreigners. In many ways their ministry had consisted of foreigners serving foreigners, for they had ministered to teachers and students from Ireland, Scotland, Wales, England, India and other parts of the world in their home and in the little English church. However, after they left, some of the Swiss who had become Christians under their influence began their own ministry in the village. For example, on the first Easter Sunday they were away, the church pianist in the village, who had been converted a few weeks earlier, conducted worship and read one of Fran's Bible studies to a group of English visitors at the church. To her surprise, she had seen English visitors heading for the church that morning—the Schaeffers had left so quickly they had forgotten to take their church service advertisements out of the hotels—so rather than disappoint them she quickly prepared a service.

Later that same year, an English travel agent wrote to the village and requested worship services in the church for tourists, so the council that had expelled the Schaeffers had to reconsider their actions. Then they voted and invited them back for English Christmas Eve services in December of

1955, and Fran and Edith continued to conduct Christmas Eve services there for more than thirty years. God continued to bring foreigners to the mountains to worship Him, and He prepared some in the village to serve Him there after the Schaeffers left. God completely defeated those who had tried to remove His truth and influence.

The Schaeffers found new happiness in their house of prayer in Huemoz, and many who visited them came to know the Lord because of their unsurpassed joy and the reality God gave them. The promise God gave Edith from Isaiah 2:2–3 did not reveal all that He had planned for them, but enough for them to take the next step. As we come to Isaiah 56:6–7, we find greater detail of God's plan for them, and these verses describe L'Abri's work from the very beginning. Francis, Edith, Priscilla, Susan and Debby made a vow and bound 'themselves to the LORD to serve him, to love the name of the LORD, and to worship him' in the Swiss Alps (Isaiah 56:6).

The Holy Spirit led them to commit their lives to creating a 'house of prayer' as they did evangelism. And when they bound themselves to serving God because the loved Him, He inspired them to demonstrate His existence by *praying* for God to send them the people to serve, by *praying* for the material and spiritual provisions they needed to serve them, by *praying* for God's plan for

151

the work and the Holy Spirit's leading day by day, and by *praying* for God to send the workers of His choice if the work grew. By the grace of God, each one has kept this vow. And each one has been willing to make the needed personal sacrifices to help those God would send them.

To demonstrate God's reality requires more than praying for *our* needs to be met. It also includes making promises to God and remaining faithful. It means choosing to keep our promises no matter what the cost, so that His mighty power can work through us to overcome our sinful habits and help others. And what the Schaeffers began in Huemoz continues to this day, as those in L'Abri maintain the house of prayer that the Lord established.

The Schaeffers did not make their vow and covenant with God impulsively, but only after God had led them so clearly that to do otherwise would have been disobedient. They avoided the trap of dedicating themselves rashly, and then later reconsidering their vows and refusing to keep them (see Proverbs 20:25). As Job did in his afflictions, they trusted in God and proved His faithfulness, realising that keeping their vows would make their prayers more effective; for, 'You will pray to him, and he will hear you, and you will fulfil your vows' (Job 22:27). As they prayed to the Lord each day, God heard them, and they fulfilled their vows as the Holy Spirit worked within them—moment by moment.

To demonstrate the importance of obeying God each day and choosing to be faithful even when it hurts, they fulfilled their 'vows to the LORD in the presence of all his people' (Psalm 116:14). Edith told the L'Abri story over and over to their guests, and each time that story became an open invitation for believers and unbelievers to examine God's faithfulness in the midst of their lives. Each time she told the story, it was a renewal of their vows. To have forsaken their vows would have done far more damage than we can comprehend.

When we study the importance of making vows to the Lord, we learn another secret of their power in prayer. Edith has written, 'Prayer is a moment-by-moment example of the reality of the validity of choice.'[1] As they prayed for their Father's provisions, they chose to trust in His promise to hear them. The Bible's promises were the evidence they needed to believe and pray that He would hear as they kept their vows. The Bible sets forth the conditions that we must fulfil to have total confidence in our prayers: '*Sacrifice thank-offerings* to God, *fulfil your vows* to the Most High, and *call upon me* in the day of trouble; I will deliver you, and you will honour me' (Psalm 50:14–15, emphasis mine). They chose to fulfil their vows. They chose to thank God for His provisions, praise

Him before others, and call upon Him in their troubles, and He delivered them and they honoured Him—because He is faithful, and they chose to keep their vows.

This pattern continued day after day. When the reality of God's presence was the most real and when the attacks of Satan were the most oppressive, they kept their vows. And when God delivered them time and again, they praised Him and demonstrated to their guests God's ability to hear and answer prayer—God created a house of prayer for all the nations.

Making vows to God because of His wonderful guidance and provision is not uncommon, especially in the Old Testament. The psalmist wrote:

> I am under vows to you, O God; I will present my thank-offerings to you. For you have delivered me from death and my feet from stumbling, that I may walk before God in the light of life . . . Then will I ever sing praise to your name and fulfil my vows day after day (Psalm 56:12–13; 61:8).

When God provided the Schaeffers with a new home in the Alps, He delivered them from stumbling and inspired them to make and keep their vows. And they have continued to praise His name day after day. Breaking vows is not uncommon, and that is one reason God taught the Schaeffers to lean upon Him daily in prayer and trust Him to help them fulfil their vows in the strength He would give.

Prayer

Dear Jesus, forgive me for any vows that I have broken, and keep me from making vows rashly. Empower me to serve You today in spite of the broken vows of the past. Give me a new beginning and new joys in the power of Your Spirit, so I can demonstrate Your faithfulness to those who will believe in You through me. Give me the ability to help others come to know You. Amen.

— 18 —

MY FATHER'S PEOPLE

Gather together and come; assemble, you fugitives from the nations. Ignorant are those who carry about idols of wood, who pray to gods that cannot save.

Isaiah 45:20

*T*he Schaeffers prayed daily for the Lord to send them the people of His choice and provide for their needs. They also asked Him to keep others away. They wanted to help true believers, confused Christians and unbelievers find the reality of God, rather than provide a free vacation home or make visitors feel as if they lived in a boarding house. They took their vow so seriously that God often protected them from wasting their time and resources on the wrong people. They looked upon each person they met as a person sent from God, and each person who knocked on their door was a special, seeking person. Unbelievers felt their love and understanding, and marvelled that God loved them enough to send them to L'Abri to be cared for, prayed for and taught the truth.

To provide for those He sent, God had to give the Schaeffers more than a $1,000 earnest payment for their home. To stay in Huemoz, they had to make a $7366 down payment on Chalet les Mélèzes by 31 May, 1955. And they had only sixty days to pray for that amount. By 22 May, they had received only $4915.69, so they continued to persevere in prayer. Only on the last day did they receive the total they needed. God had motivated 156 people to send them money. God's evident display of faithfulness encouraged them to move ahead, and Fran resigned from his Mission Board on 5 June to *officially* begin L'Abri.

They bought their home and Fran resigned, *before* they knew whether or not the government would allow them to stay in Switzerland! They prayed and trusted that God, who had met their needs day by day and who had led them to buy their chalet, would not disappoint them by allowing the government to force them back to America in defeat. And on 21 June, they received their permit to stay. God saved them once again.

Over the years of L'Abri, God has demonstrated that He is more than able to save both materially and spiritually, unlike the idols that many embrace. Certainly, God demonstrated His deep concern for their work when He motivated more than 150 people to send small amounts of money to buy their home, rather than using only a handful of people with larger gifts. Since 1955, L'Abri has been sustained by small, sacrificial gifts, and has only received large gifts for very special needs—perhaps to demonstrate that God can work in a variety of ways, using both poor and rich Christians in answer to prayer.

The Schaeffers prayed for God's provision to care for God's people. And in their first twelve months, they had 187 guests. One of those guests was John Sandri, who became a Christian and one of their first workers—one of the Lord's provisions. Later, he married Priscilla, and they went to Covenant Seminary in St Louis to prepare for further work in L'Abri.

L'Abri never had too much money to help the hundreds who came, and by December of 1957 they desperately needed $2,000 to meet their household expenses. In answer to fervent prayer, they received $2,000.35. God usually brought in little amounts day by day to show each visitor and worker that *He* was providing for them. God showed believers and unbelievers that He answered prayer, that He provided their home, that He gave them both physical and spiritual food, and they praised Him. God knew who was coming and how to care for each one. God knew what prayers to answer and when to answer them in order to have the greatest positive effect on the greatest number of people—that some might come to saving faith and others have their faith renewed.

As the Schaeffers prayed for the Lord to send the people of His choice and give them the means to care for them physically, they also prayed for the means to help them spiritually. They could teach the truth of the Bible intellectually, and demonstrate the power of God and faithful living, but only the Holy Spirit could give people an understanding heart. They took very seriously the example of Paul, who wrote: 'I pray also that the eyes of your heart may be enlightened in order that you may know the hope to which he has called you, the riches of his glorious inheritance in the saints' (Ephesians 1:18).

The Schaeffers spent much time in prayer, because they had to pray for many things. They had to pray for God to send the people of His choice. They had to pray for the right words to be shared at just the right time. They had to pray for the right accommodation for those who came as well as the food to serve—because those who came were their guests. They had to pray for the Holy Spirit to open people's minds to receive the truth. And as the drug culture advanced and people's minds were clouded by false ideas and religions, they had to pray with real fervency that the Holy Spirit would lift the cloud and use their feeble efforts to lead these troubled people to the Saviour.

The work of L'Abri would have been easier, if the Schaeffers had simply stayed in their mountain home and talked to a few people who came. However, as students from various places came to L'Abri, became Christians, and returned to school, they wanted weekly Bible studies and discussions to help them grow spiritually and remain firm in their faith. And they wanted to introduce nonbelievers to Dr Schaeffer and the truth he taught. Within a few of months, Dr Schaeffer began travelling to Milan, Lausanne and Basel to hold three-hour Bible classes and answer the questions of new Christians and unbelievers.

L'Abri moved beyond classes in cafés, and on 11 March, 1958, the Schaeffers received 250 English pounds to begin a L'Abri in England at some point in the future. That same year, Ranald Macaulay travelled to the Swiss L'Abri, having met Fran at Cambridge. Another one of the Lord's provisions,

161

he would marry Susan and together they would eventually start a resident English L'Abri.

To meet all the demands upon them, God sent them the people of His choice to help them, and as He sent workers the need for everyone's provisions increased. In addition to leading sinners to salvation, Fran had to train helpers and workers to assist in the work, and teach them how to share the truth in the context of the spiritual awakening going on in their midst. As more came than one chalet could hold, they had to pray for more housing. And as they outgrew the village, they had to pray for God to provide other places in other countries, so that L'Abri could go there should He choose. They only sought God's plan for the work, and the work grew so quickly that by 1960 Edith's mother was mailing out 1300 L'Abri family letters.

Living by faith and prayer alone takes a tremendous amount of work and requires great physical and spiritual strength. The Schaeffers did not pray for God's provision and the people of His choice just to do something pious to please God. From their hearts, they knew their limitations and faults. They knew that only the Holy Spirit could sort through all the people and their needs, and send them those He had prepared to serve. As hundreds demanded more of their time and energy, God gave them the strength and endurance to keep on and show Christian grace under the pressures of more difficult and strenuous work.

Prayer

Dear Father, help me count the cost of living by faith. If I begin this way of living by faith alone, keep me from turning back or being a poor example. For Jesus' sake. Amen.

19

LIVING BEFORE OTHERS

I want men everywhere to lift up holy hands in prayer, without anger or disputing.

1 Timothy 2:8

Through L'Abri, the Schaeffer family demonstrated God's power to change outward things and provide for their needs in answer to prayer. And they also demonstrated God's power to transform a person's life by a daily moulding of their character into the image of Jesus Christ. God would require them to exercise all the Christian graces before a watching world, before people who had become sceptical, cynical and disillusioned.

After they began L'Abri, both Christians and non-Christians would watch how Fran controlled or lost his temper when provoked, and then see what he would do if his temper flared. Believers and nonbelievers would see how the Schaeffer family reacted when their patience was tried. They would see how the family dealt with people's flaws and mistakes; especially those that were not character flaws but personality differences. And sometimes unbelievers would intentionally goad them to test their Christian character and commitment. The whole family lived under the day-by-day scrutiny of those they were trying to help and of those who were training to be helpers. And when some became workers and began to participate in the practical decision-making and share in the growing responsibility and pressures of helping more and more people, they all had to learn how to deal with conflict and diversity in the spirit of Jesus Christ.

So the L'Abri family also prayed for God to give each one the reality of spiritual growth and the ability to demonstrate God's grace to overcome all temptations. They did not just pray for God to work visible miracles in the material things, without also praying for God to work in the spiritual realm and build Christian character.

L'Abri became a complete work by demonstrating the Lordship of Christ over all, especially over our moral life.

When Dr Schaeffer told unbelievers how to be saved, he said they needed to bow both metaphysically and morally. First, they needed to know God: the Father, Son and Holy Spirit, and receive the Bible as God's Word to them and the world. They needed to turn from their arrogance and desire for personal autonomy, and accept themselves as creatures created in the image of God. They needed to believe the truth about reality and themselves as revealed by God through His Word and reason.

Second, they needed to understand that their problem was basically moral and spiritual rather than physical or metaphysical. They had rebelled and sinned against the Creator of all, the rightful Lord of the universe. They had disregarded His laws and set up their own standards to follow. They were rebels and needed to bow morally by accepting their moral guilt, admitting they were sinners, and asking Jesus Christ to forgive them and save them on the basis of His atoning death. They needed to resolve every day to live under the Lordship of Jesus Christ and obey Him in all things. If they sinned, they needed to go to Him as Saviour and ask Him to forgive them and cleanse them by His blood. Each day, often many times a day, they needed to ask Jesus to give them the power of the Holy Spirit to live an obedient and submissive life—to follow Him wherever He led.

However, much of Francis and Edith Schaeffer's teaching in these two areas would have meant very little if they had not also tried to live before others on the basis of their teaching. With more than 2,000 pages of published auto-biographical materials from the Schaeffers, we know their lives in relation to their private teaching and many books, and these pages do not call attention to them as much as to the Lord they tried to glorify by their work. In their works, even as they revealed personal things about themselves, they always tried to point people to God, so that He would receive the credit for everything He accomplished through them. They never pointed to themselves as examples of morality and purity; they pointed people to God as the source of all good and quietly demonstrated that the Holy Spirit could make Christians into examples of true holiness. Hundreds who have lived or worked with them in L'Abri can testify to the fact that they lived exemplary Christian lives: they practised what they preached.

Only our living with consistency day by day will help many overcome their cynicism and scepticism about the validity of the Christian faith. Even though those in L'Abri have struggled against the world, the flesh and the devil (as all of us must in this life), they have lived consistently with their teaching from the Word of God. They have demonstrated the possibility and the reality of a moral transformation through the Truth and Spirit of God, and if they had not done this, their work would not have been so highly effective in helping others live likewise. Because the Schaeffers lived as consistent Christians, their work will last longer than their lives, much as the influence of Hudson Taylor and George Müller has continued and for the same reasons.

In the Sermon on the Mount, Jesus told His disciples:

You are the light of the world. A city on a hill cannot be hidden. Neither do people light a lamp and put it under a bowl. Instead they put it on its stand, and it gives light to everyone in the house. In the same way, let your light shine before men, that they may see your good deeds and praise your Father in heaven (Matthew 5:14–16).

The Schaeffers did this in the most difficult way possible: they vowed that anyone who knocked on their door seeking spiritual help could live in their home if there were room, and they would demonstrate the reality of God in their

169

presence, not by working signs and wonders, but by demonstrating true spirituality, praying for God's daily provisions, and giving honest answers to honest questions.[1]

Anyone who has had a guest stay in their home too long, whether family or welcome friend, has only a small idea of what the pressures are like to have complete strangers (some unkempt and unwashed, some having their minds deranged from drugs or demons, some obnoxious and unable to get along with anyone) living in your home day after day, and evaluating your every move until the early hours of almost every morning as tough philosophical, theological and biblical questions are asked. Only the wonderful grace of God has kept L'Abri workers demonstrating the life-transforming power of Jesus Christ in these situations to those who desperately need such transformation through a personal faith in Him.[2]

The Schaeffers and those in L'Abri have much power in prayer because they live holy lives, not in their own strength, but in a moment-by-moment dependence on the Holy Spirit. For us to have power in prayer we need to be able to raise holy hands to our Heavenly Father. We must take ourselves to Christ for cleansing and come into the presence of God in His name and righteousness, and that means that we must take very seriously every aspect of our thought life and outward life. God looks upon the heart as well as our outward actions; however, others may be attracted to or repelled from the Christian faith after observing our behaviour and treatment of them and others.

Prayer

Dear Heavenly Father, I praise You today for all You can do in the lives of those who trust in You. Thank You for providing Jesus Christ as the Way of life and holy living. I pray that You will transform me into Your image and use me today. Amen.

20

HEARING THE PRAYERS OF UNBELIEVERS

*And without faith it is impossible to please God,
because anyone who comes to him must believe
that he exists and that he rewards those who
earnestly seek him.*

Hebrews 11:6

God loves His creation and every living creature.
As our Creator and Governor, God meets the needs
of everyone, and every gift anyone receives

ultimately comes from our loving and caring God. In this way, God shows His love for His enemies as well as His friends. And He does not require any more of us than He does of Himself. Jesus commanded His followers: 'But I tell you: Love your enemies and pray for those who persecute you, that you may be sons of your Father in heaven. He causes his sun to rise on the evil and the good, and sends rain on the righteous and the unrighteous' (Matthew 5:44–45). When we love and bless our enemies our moral character is similar to the character of God and we are truly His children.

The Apostle Paul confirmed this principle of actively loving our enemies when he preached to those who worshipped idols: 'Yet [God] has not left himself without testimony: He has shown kindness by giving you rain from heaven and crops in their seasons; he provides you with plenty of food and fills your hearts with joy' (Acts 14:17). God's goodness to all is a testimony to His character, and may lead some to recognise His work in the world and come to believe in Him. If we live in accordance with the character of our Heavenly Father, we bring credit to God and honour Him before others, and our testimony about Him takes on greater credibility.

As Jesus hung on the cross, He prayed for His enemies and practised the love He preached.

When one of the robbers who hung beside Him saw Him bless His cruel enemies instead of curse them, he repented and was saved (Luke 23:34, 47–48). The way God's Son died as a human being demonstrated the extent of God's love for His enemies, and made the atonement the greatest event in human history. As Paul wrote, 'God demonstrates his own love for us in this: While we were still sinners, Christ died for us' (Romans 5:8).

God wants us to act like His sons and daughters in this age of grace, and He calls us to represent His character and loving approach towards the wicked. We must help them find God and meet many of their other needs. Just as God blesses both the righteous and the unrighteous by giving them sun and rain for their crops, so we need to love, pray for and seek to do *all the good we wisely can* to help others regardless of their character. As the Schaeffers practised love for all, they especially demonstrated God's love for unbelievers. For the first time, some who had been raised in the church all their lives and had rejected Christ saw how a group of Christians should love one another and treat the unrighteous. They saw Christian love practised as well as preached and that led them to consider the gospel's claims once again. When they learned about the true character of God by observing how His children acted, many came to believe in and worship the true God.

Yet, regarding prayer, we cannot say that God treats believers and unbelievers in exactly the same way. In the Bible, God revealed the conditions that we need to fulfil to have assurance of receiving His answers to our prayers; and wicked, unbelieving people do not fulfil these conditions. For example, faith is a condition for pleasing God. And confidence in prayer depends on the conditions of pleasing God, and believing that He exists and rewards those who earnestly seek Him (Hebrews 11:6).

The cries of the wicked are not the same as the prayers of the righteous. Because God loves everyone, He will sometimes answer the cries of the wicked, but this is totally different from answering the prayers of the righteous. Just as we would try to save a family that screamed inside a burning house, without first evaluating their character to see if they were worthy of our efforts, time and time again God shows His mercy and redeeming power by rescuing rebellious and unbelieving people from tragedies or from suffering the full consequences of their disobedience when they cry out to Him. But because of their rebellion, too often they will not acknowledge God's providential care for them or come to saving faith.

The Bible does not give the wicked any reason to believe that God will answer their prayers.

Indeed, we discover that when the Israelites continued to live in sin, they could not find God when they prayed. When the prophet Hosea called them to repent, he revealed a principle that not only applies to the twelve tribes of Israel, but to every person who is guilty of rebelling against God: 'Israel's arrogance testifies against them; the Israelites, even Ephraim, stumble in their sin; Judah also stumbles with them. When they go with their flocks and herds to seek the LORD, they will not find him; he has withdrawn himself from them' (Hosea 5:5–6). Sin separates us from God and keeps us from praying effectively. The Psalmist also recognised the destructive power of sin with respect to prayer:

> Come and listen, all you who fear God; let me tell you what he has done for me. I cried out to him with my mouth; his praise was on my tongue. If I had cherished sin in my heart, the Lord would not have listened; but God has surely listened and heard my voice in prayer. Praise be to God, who has not rejected my prayer or withheld his love from me! (Psalm 66:16–20)

To have confidence that God will answer us when we pray, we must go to God in Christ Jesus, the Way God has provided. But we must not simply 'name His Name' as a magical formula, thinking that will move God. Going to God in Jesus Christ includes asking Him to forgive us and cleanse us from all unrighteousness, to make us worthy to come into His presence. Otherwise, we pray with presumption and have no assurance that God will hear us and answer our prayers. Failure to recognise this vital principle, after they have believed in and claimed other promises from God in the Bible as they have prayed, has led some wicked people who thought they trusted in God to eventually reject God and prayer because He did not come near.

God will sometimes hear the calls of distress by wicked and sinful people, but He has not promised to hear their prayers. Prayer is far more than a distress signal. Regarding true prayer, the Scriptures state clearly: 'The LORD detests the sacrifice of the wicked, but the prayer of the upright pleases him . . . The LORD is far from the wicked but he hears the prayer of the righteous' (Proverbs 15:8, 29).

If we have practised sin and run away from God, God encourages us to return: 'You will seek me and find me when you seek me with all your heart' (Jeremiah 29:13). To seek God with *all* our heart means that we do not cherish sin in our hearts. We must turn from all known sin to seek after Him. God has promised that we will find

Him *if* we turn from sin and earnestly seek Him with a heart to obey Him when we find Him.

Prayer

Dear Heavenly Father, reveal to me any sin or love for sin that may be keeping me from You or knowing by experience that Your face shines upon me. I do repent of all my sins now, and ask that You will forgive me for all my unrighteousness. I bow before Jesus Christ and acknowledge Him as my Lord and Saviour. Thank you for drawing me towards You by the power of Your Holy Spirit and saving my soul for Jesus' sake. Amen.

21

DAYS OF FASTING AND PRAYER

But the time will come when the bridegroom will be taken from them; in those days they will fast.
Luke 5:35

God taught the Schaeffers to set aside every Monday as a Day of Prayer for L'Abri. Edith would begin the day by teaching those staying at L'Abri about prayer, and giving some examples of the answers to prayer they had received to encourage everyone to persevere in prayer. She made a prayer list with some Bible verses at the top, so that people could begin praying after first hearing from God and thinking about how they could pray in the context of His Word. Then she listed some of the needs of others and L'Abri so that each person could pray privately, but in unity with all the rest. These prayer requests might be for the individual guidance and protection of others, for someone to embrace the truth of the gospel, or for some specific needs of the community.

In this way, the Schaeffers taught those at L'Abri that God intended prayer to be centred on Him and intercessory, rather than primarily focused on our self-centred needs. And they also emphasised that prayer could be for things in the material realm as well as the spiritual. At Susan's suggestion, Edith divided each Monday's prayer list into twenty-eight half-hour periods. Then people could sign up to pray for half an hour or more so that the entire day would be covered in prayer.

The L'Abri Family Prayer Letters are similar to these lists, so the Praying Family of L'Abri can join in the Monday Day of Prayer or pray throughout the week wherever they live. Beginning in June of 1955, Edith began sending Prayer Letters to those who had promised to pray specifically for L'Abri each day. At first, she sent out about twenty-five letters, but soon the numbers grew to a few hundred.

Sometimes, those in L'Abri were amazed to learn about prayer groups that prayed specifically for them, groups they knew nothing about for several years. For example, from their travels to Cambridge, England, in 1967, they learned of eight students who met together each Tuesday for breakfast to pray for L'Abri and especially for its purchase of Chalet les Sapins so that they would have more room for guests and students. This group also prayed for the expansion of L'Abri into their own country.

God's teaching those at L'Abri about prayer through the Monday Day of Prayer remains highly effective, because people set aside time to spend with God alone in the context of a larger number of people praying with one heart for many things. After seeing much persevering prayer, those new to L'Abri begin to recognise God's answers to prayer and praise Him for His love and faithfulness. Sometimes God sends His answer that very day, but usually in the days ahead, in order to teach people to pray and not give up. God works out the timing of each answer to encourage different people and meet the unique needs they have for an intelligent faith. Sometimes He answers the specific prayer of one person for a specific amount of money to be received on a specific day to meet a specific need of that person and to encourage everyone in L'Abri to keep on praying.

On 30 July, 1955, L'Abri also began setting aside one day each year as a Special Day of Fasting and Prayer. These special days were similar to the Monday Day of Prayer, except the whole day was dedicated to prayer alone, and only a light meal was left out on a table for those who physically needed to eat or for those who chose not to fast.

Jesus said His disciples would fast after He returned to heaven, and the early Church fasted and prayed and left us their example to follow. Through prayer and fasting, God revealed to the early Christians who they should commission to serve Him and the Church. In the book of Acts we read: 'While they were worshipping the Lord and fasting, the Holy Spirit said, "Set apart for me Barnabas and Saul for the work to which I have called them" ' (Acts 13:2). Barnabas and Saul continued this practice. In the churches they founded, they only commissioned elders after fasting and prayer: 'Paul and Barnabas appointed elders for them in each church and, with prayer and fasting, committed them to the Lord, in whom they had put their trust' (Acts 14:23).

Those in L'Abri sometimes fasted more than one day a year. In times of crisis or for special needs, such as the need for more room or food for desperate seekers, they would call for another Day of Fasting and Prayer or individuals would fast quietly and privately. If the need were especially grave, they would sometimes have two or more days of fasting in one month. They were not being legalistic when setting special days for worship and prayer. They loved God and were calling upon Him, because He had promised to give special attention to their prayers when they came to Him in some of the special ways He has prescribed.

Fasting indicates to God that we are serious about Him and His ability to help us and others. Fasting indicates that we are willing to deny ourselves to follow Him. Fasting indicates that we are at the end of our ability to meet our own needs and recognise that He is the only One who can help. There is nothing meritorious in fasting, and God does not give us 'extra credit' for fasting and prayer. Times of fasting and prayer are opportunities to draw near to God and prepare ourselves to receive Him when He draws near to us. Fasting simply tells God (and sometimes others) that we are serious about serving Him and Him only, and that we are relying upon Him and Him only to do His work in our lives in His way. Fasting should indicate our absolute submission to the will of God. And it can reveal to us any rebellious spirit that we may still have within us. As we pray and fast, we must continually remind God and ourselves, 'Thy will be done,' and be satisfied with the answer to prayer God gives—whether He gives us the exact letter or only the spirit of our request.

Days of Fasting and Prayer should indicate to God and others that we have supreme confidence in Him. Observing these special days does not mean that we are trying to manipulate or extract blessings from a stingy God. Rather, they indicate the value we place on spending time with God, and show that we want to do all that we do in submission to His will.

Just as the early Church did not dare to commission anyone to service without spending time in prayer and fasting, today, prayer and fasting indicates to God that we do not want to do anything but His will and that we are willing to take the time to find out what He wants. Fasting indicates that we are willing to sacrifice our comforts and make any other sacrifices that God may require to further His Kingdom on earth. Fasting and prayer indicate to God that we delight in being with Him more than anyone or anything else, and that time spent with Him and the spiritual food He feeds us is of far more value to us than the material foods we eat daily. Fasting should lead us to recommit ourselves to God and assure Him and us that we have no other will than that His will be done.

Prayer

Dear Heavenly Father, show me when I need to spend some special times in fasting and prayer. Help me to always put You above the desires of my flesh. Use my days of fasting to free me from any cravings or unwholesome desires that are keeping me from desiring Your presence, knowing You fully, receiving Your guidance, or being an effective servant. Keep me from thinking that You owe me something on the basis of anything I have done. Refresh me with Your presence. In Jesus' name. Amen.

CONFIDENCE IN PRAYER AND OUR CONSCIENCE

> *Dear friends, if our hearts do not condemn us, we have confidence before God and receive from him anything we ask, because we obey his commands and do what pleases him.*
>
> 1 John 3:21–22

Dr Schaeffer taught that for Christians prayer in its simplest form was asking, 'Up, Daddy, up.' Through faith in Jesus Christ, God becomes our

Heavenly Father, and since Jesus said 'Abba, Father' when He prayed, so can His brothers and sisters (Mark 14:36). The Apostle Paul confirmed this when he wrote: 'For you did not receive a spirit that makes you a slave again to fear, but you received the Spirit of sonship. And by him we cry, "Abba, Father" ' (Romans 8:15).

'Abba' means 'Daddy', and is a child's name for father. Christians must come to God as His little children, humbly seeking God's will for their lives and expecting their Heavenly Father to meet their real needs. In the Sermon on the Mount, Jesus encouraged His disciples to seek only the best from God and assured them that God would give them only good and perfect gifts (Matthew 7:9–11).

Daily prayer, and especially days of fasting, give us the opportunity to show God or discover for ourselves whether God or what He gives is most important to us. Do we fast and pray *only* for God's gifts and our daily bread? Or do we fast and pray because we love God and delight in being with Him? Do we always go to our Heavenly Father with our hands out for the things He can give? Or do we most often go with our hands up, asking just to sit in His presence and enjoy His fellowship? Times of fasting and prayer enable God to show us the true state of hearts: do we love God for who He is, or just for what He gives?

In true prayer, we must lift up holy hands to God. Just as an earthly father wearing a white, starched shirt would prefer not to pick up his child when his hands are muddy, and would ask him to go wash them first, so our Heavenly Father wants us to come to Him with hands that have been cleansed from all sin. And He has provided the One who will do the cleansing, even His own Son, Jesus Christ. In our prayers, we need to ask Jesus to create a clean heart within us and cleanse us from all unrighteousness, so we are fit to come into our Heavenly Father's presence (Psalm 51:10). However, this is not a magic act. Jesus expects us to repent of our sins, to forsake all known sins, and to ask Him to free us from bondage to any sins. Jesus expects us to ask Him to fill us with the Holy Spirit so that we are empowered to overcome all temptations moment by moment.

When we obey God and do what pleases Him, our hearts will not condemn us and we will have confidence in prayer. Long times spent in prayer will enable God to reveal to us the true state of our hearts. In 1 John 3:21–22, the word 'heart' means 'conscience'. If our *conscience* does not condemn us, then we can come to God in prayer with the confidence that He will hear us and give us our requests. A clear conscience will give us confidence when we pray.

God taught the Schaeffers and others through

L'Abri that they needed to obey Him and pray often each day to keep a clean conscience and always to have clean hands when they prayed. This meant they needed to pray moment by moment for the knowledge of God's will and the power to do it. One of the best ways to maintain a clean conscience is to keep reminding ourselves, 'The only thing I want is to please God and bring Him happiness'; and then to ask God, 'Show me what you want me to do, and I will do it without hesitation. Empower me, so you will be glorified by my actions.' To maintain a good conscience, we need to dedicate ourselves each day to doing all the will of God we know without a hint of rebellion, and do all that we have committed ourselves to do before the Lord.

Francis and Edith Schaeffer were not legalistic. Because they truly loved God, they were determined to keep a clean conscience even in the little things. In this way, they knew they would also always have access to God, especially in times of need or with special concerns for others. Because they loved God and sought to please Him, they wanted to fulfil *all* the conditions that God has set forth in the Bible as reasons for answering prayer. For example, even now, if Edith writes a letter and says that she will pray for someone, she stops at that moment so that she and her secretary can pray for that person. In this way, times of simply dictating letters become little prayer meetings.[1]

God taught the Schaeffers to be faithful in the small things so that they would be prepared for the awesome responsibilities of L'Abri. Jesus said, 'Whoever can be trusted with very little can also be trusted with much, and whoever is dishonest with very little will also be dishonest with much' (Luke 16:10). In founding L'Abri, God knew Francis and Edith Schaeffer could be trusted with much, because over the years they had proved faithful in the little things and were willing always to have a 'little' work if that were God's will for them.

The Apostle Paul had power in prayer because he too kept a good conscience. When on trial, 'Paul looked straight at the Sanhedrin and said,"My brothers, I have fulfilled my duty to God in all good conscience to this day" ' (Acts 23:1). And later he declared, 'I strive always to keep my conscience clear before God and man' (Acts 24:16). When he wrote to the Christians in Rome, he said that he depended on his conscience and the Holy Spirit to commend or condemn his behaviour: 'I speak the truth in Christ—I am not lying, my conscience confirms it in the Holy Spirit' (Romans 9:1). To maintain an open communication with God, we must seek to do His will not because we fear punishment, but because we love Him and want to keep a clear conscience (Romans 13:5).

And yet, the Bible teaches that our conscience will not be our final judge, for Paul wrote, 'My conscience is clear, but that does not make me innocent. It is the Lord who judges me' (1 Corinthians 4:4).

Our prayers must include asking God to give us a tender conscience—even in the small things—so we will not disobey Him in anything or commit any sins of omission. We cannot rely only on our conscience, but need to ask the Lord to show us His estimation of our character so we can make needed changes. To have power in prayer, we need to believe that neither the Lord nor our conscience condemns us, and that we have clean hands and pure motives when asking 'Up, Daddy, up.' Spending real time in prayer will enable God to show us if we have any impure or mixed motives, so that we can make unselfish requests that He will honour.

We will miss the lessons God wants us to learn if we do not take this seriously:

Now this is our boast: Our conscience testifies that we have conducted ourselves in the world, and especially in our relations with you, in the holiness and sincerity that are from God. We have done so not according to worldly wisdom but according to God's grace . . . Rather, we have renounced secret and shameful ways; we do not use deception, nor do we distort the word of God. On the contrary, by setting forth the truth plainly we commend ourselves to every man's conscience in the sight of God (2 Corinthians 1:12; 4:2).

Prayer

Dear Heavenly Father, help me to spend time in self-evaluation so that I can see myself as You see me. Help me to live each day so that my conscience will be a more reliable guide. In Jesus' name. Amen.

— 23 —

PRAYER AND RIGHTEOUSNESS

*Is any one of you in trouble? He should pray. Is
anyone happy? Let him sing songs of praise. Is
any one of you sick? He should call the elders of
the church to pray over him and anoint him with
oil in the name of the Lord . . . Therefore confess
your sins to each other and pray for each other so
that you may be healed. The prayer of a righteous
man is powerful and effective.*

James 5:13–14, 16

*O*nly the prayers of righteous people are powerful and effective. To be powerful and effective in prayer, we must be righteous. Jesus Christ makes us righteous, and we are righteous 'in Christ'. However, being 'in Christ' must be relational, and not just positional. To pray effectively, we must actually be in a righteous relationship with God through Christ, and not claim to be in some mystical 'position' that releases us from the responsibility of acting rightly. To be 'in Christ' means that the life-transforming power of Jesus Christ is working within us to help us live according to the revealed will of God. Too many people have ineffective prayer lives, because they think they can live in sin and substitute a so-called 'position' in Christ for maintaining a righteous, obedient relationship with God in Christ.

The Apostle Paul wrote: 'There is now no condemnation for those who are in Christ Jesus' (Romans 8:1). And he indicated that being 'in Christ' is the same as being a Christian (Romans 16:7). Since our attitudes and behaviour can be 'tested and approved in Christ', our righteousness must be more than some simple position of being 'in Christ' (Romans 16:10). Paul wrote to the Corinthians, 'Therefore, if anyone is in Christ, he is a new creation; the old has gone, the new has come!' (2 Corinthians 5:17). New creatures in

Christ have a new spiritual power within them, and they will behave differently from the way they used to: 'in Christ' God gives us the power of the Holy Spirit to act righteously instead of being powerless in the face of temptation and continually practising sin.

The book of Revelation confirms this interpretation, because in it we see Jesus commended and worshipped for His righteous acts: 'Who will not fear you, O Lord, and bring glory to your name? For you alone are holy. All nations will come and worship before you, for your righteous acts have been revealed' (Revelation 15:4). Jesus Christ will be worshipped because of His character, and the actions that flowed from that character. A part of our ministry demands that we commend and reveal God's character to an unbelieving world by our actions as well as our words, so that some will believe and worship Him. God led many people from many nations to L'Abri, because He could demonstrate His righteous acts through the Schaeffers and their workers as they prayed and told the truth about Him.

We also read in Revelation that *our* righteous acts are important to God. In heaven, the white linen garments of the saints (Christians) symbolise *their* righteous acts: 'Fine linen, bright and clean, was given her to wear' (Revelation 19:8). (Fine linen stands for the righteous acts of the saints.) In heaven, God will reveal the lasting value of our righteous deeds, and demonstrate that our holiness depended upon and flowed from our being in Christ. Only in this way will our Lord and Saviour receive all the glory for our righteous behaviour in this life. *Our righteousness must be real in Christ*, and consciously sought through Bible study, prayer and reliance upon the Holy Spirit to work within us. We must not think that some 'position' of being 'in Christ' can substitute for the righteous acts that God requires us to do in His strength. To misunderstand what it means to be 'in Christ' will rob us of our power in prayer.

James also recognised that Christians will sin from time to time. They will sometimes succumb to the temptations of the world, the flesh and the devil. They will sometimes hurt God and one another through their sins. When this happens, James says that we must confess our sins to God and those we have harmed. We need to seek the forgiveness of those we have harmed and make amends whenever possible. When we confess our sins and forgive one another, we restore the power of prayer that we have lost because of sin. The Scriptures clearly teach that we will not have power in prayer, if we will not forsake our sins, confess our sins if we sin, and forgive those who sin against us.

Intellectually believing some facts about Jesus Christ and His life and work will never be a substitute for our actually loving God and others. John wrote that we must believe in Jesus and keep His commands:

And this is his command: to believe in the name of his Son, Jesus Christ, and to love one another as he commanded us. *Those who obey his commands live in him, and he in them.* And this is how we know that he lives in us: We know it by the Spirit he gave us (1 John 3:23–24, emphasis mine).

The Holy Spirit bears testimony that we are children of God, but the Holy Spirit will never lead people to think they can live in open rebellion to the commands of God and have Jesus living within them. Christians are in a covenant relationship with God in Jesus Christ, and God will discipline His children to lead them to live righteously in Christ Jesus and remain in a right relationship with Him and others.

As the Schaeffers worked and witnessed in L'Abri, and as they kept an open home so that anyone could evaluate their lives and see whether or not they lived consistently with their teachings, they tried to live in the spirit of the early apostles. They prayed for God's guidance and strength to enable them to practise biblical Christianity in the power of the Holy Spirit moment by moment. They could have said with the Apostle Paul: 'Since, then, we know what it is to fear the Lord, we try to persuade men. What we are is plain to God, and I hope it is also plain to your conscience' (2 Corinthians 5:11). By living open and transparent lives before the world, their teaching had a moral urgency and persuasiveness not available to those who live in hypocrisy.[1]

As they tried to talk with others about the good news of Jesus, their lives day by day commended their teaching, but they could not have lived with this type of consistency if they had not prayed for the Holy Spirit to work within them to overcome the many temptations they faced. And they would not have been effective in prayer if they had not tried to read the Bible, so that God's Word would inform their conscience and make it so tender that they could live day by day in a way that would not offend God or their conscience.

Rather than pointing to themselves as examples, Francis and Edith Schaeffer let their lives and prayers speak for themselves. And others recognised that they prayed effectively because they honoured God by their obedience moment by moment in the power of the Holy Spirit. When they founded L'Abri and asked others to pray with them for their work, they could have honestly written: 'Pray for us. We are sure that we have a clear conscience and desire to live honourably in every way' (Hebrews 13:18). They prayed from a heart of love for God and others, and this overcame any tendency towards legalism and gave them power in prayer.

Prayer

Dear Heavenly Father, help me learn about what You have made available for me in Christ Jesus. I know that the only righteous acts acceptable to You are those that flow from faith in Jesus Christ by Your grace. Fill me with Your loving Holy Spirit, and enable me to love more and more as You have commanded. Amen.

24

PRAYER AND SELF-EXAMINATION

With this in mind, we constantly pray for you, that our God may count you worthy of his calling, and that by his power he may fulfil every good purpose of yours and every act prompted by your faith. We pray this so that the name of our Lord Jesus may be glorified in you, and you in him, according to the grace of our God and the Lord Jesus Christ.

2 Thessalonians 1:11–12

*L*iving by faith and prayer does not guarantee that everything will go smoothly and that we will receive immediate results from every prayer. When we learn about the prayer lives of the Schaeffers and others at L'Abri, we do see God sometimes answering a prayer on the very day they prayed. In most of these cases, God had prepared the answer in advance, and then by His Spirit inspired them to pray for that thing or a specific amount of money, so that He could assure them that He was endorsing their ministry by meeting their needs. But if some begin to think that God will always automatically or mechanically work this immediately in answer to their prayers, or that He answers immediately because they are special or more faithful or more holy or more Spirit-filled, or have placed God under obligation to them, God may need to teach them that His answers always flow from His grace, by delaying His answers and using other ways to humble them.

And yet, Paul wrote that we should pray and work so that God will find us and others 'worthy of His calling'. Our days of prayer or fasting should include our pleading for God's help so that we and others 'may live a life worthy of the Lord and may please him in every way: bearing fruit in every good work, growing in the knowledge of

God' (Colossians 1:10). When God delays in answering our prayers, we need to persist in prayer, but also examine our attitudes and actions to see whether or not we are still in the faith.

Days of fasting should include obeying Paul's admonition: 'Examine yourselves to see whether you are in the faith; test yourselves. Do you not realise that Christ Jesus is in you—unless, of course, you fail the test?' (2 Corinthians 13:5). If we think our prayers are not being heard by God, we need to examine our lives and ask ourselves:

- Am I still living worthy of His calling?
- In making these requests, am I asking God to fulfil good purposes?
- Are my actions and prayers prompted by faith?
- Do I really want the Lord Jesus glorified in me?
- Do I have good reasons to pray for this *courageously* (see 1 Chronicles 17:25)?

We need to be careful, however, that we do not think all delays to our prayers indicate we are unworthy or have committed some great sin and that God is punishing us by being slow to grant our requests. L'Abri has sometimes gone for more than a month with funds so low that worker allowances could not be paid, and more water had to be added to the soup to feed hungry students and guests; and yet, this has not meant that someone in the community had sinned or that they needed to find 'the Achan in the camp' (see Joshua 7 and 22:20). They used the delays to draw closer to the Lord and each other, and encouraged one another to spend more time in prayer. Some would sign up to pray for two hours instead of thirty minutes, so the delays brought great spiritual blessings.

In some cases, after weeks of prayer, God would inspire the one who prayed the extra hour to pray for a specific amount of money and then send that amount in that day's mail. God would use the delay and His specific answer in order to encourage those He was teaching to persevere in prayer and look for other reasons for His delays rather than think they lacked faith or had sinned.

In the Scriptures, we learn that Daniel was a righteous man who prayed several times a day, but at least on one occasion he had to pray for twenty-one days to get his answer because a demon had wrestled with the angel God had sent with His answer (see Daniel 10). We need to remember that with every prayer we enter a spiritual battle, and many delays will have no relationship at all to our faith or character. The book of Job also teaches this lesson, for even though Job was blameless he suffered.

As we think of why we may need to persist in prayer for certain things, sometimes for years, we need to remember that God does not always prepare people in advance to meet our needs in answer to prayer. Indeed, a speedy response may be the exception to the rule with regard to prayer. Otherwise, our prayers could lose their significance. Many times God will only move people to answer our prayers *as* we pray and as we pray more prayers. In some mysterious way, the process He uses to motivate people, and the number of people He motivates to send money or food or clothing or books or whatever we need, depends on how many prayers people pray and for how long they pray and how many people actually pray.

All of this has some significance in the spiritual battle that we do not see clearly. When God answers prayers, He builds up faith and encourages as many people as possible, and His delays often allow Him to bless and influence far more people than He otherwise could. So, even as we pray in desperation at times, we can praise God and ask Him to use the times of delay to bring more glory to Himself and bless more people when we receive the results of our prayers. Through delays, God teaches how important our prayers really are in the supernatural realm and in history.

Sometimes our answers to prayer are delayed, because those God is motivating are refusing to obey His leading. The sin of others, rather than our sins or the community's sins, may be the cause of our continuing to suffer. And yet, the Holy Spirit needs to point out this failure to someone rather than our saying, 'Our suffering or lack is the result of you not giving us your money.' L'Abri has demonstrated that the Holy Spirit is perfectly capable of moving people to help us without our trying to make people feel guilty or manipulate them in other ways.

Sometimes God wants to meet our needs differently from the way we expect, and on His timetable instead of ours. When L'Abri desperately needed more room, they prayed for about $17,000 to buy Chalet les Sapins, which was very close to them. They had several days of fasting and prayer in one month alone, but God said, 'Not yet.' He allowed a group with Hindu-type teachings to buy it instead. But the very day L'Abri learned it had been sold to someone else, they received a cheque for $2,000 'for more room', which they used to enlarge Chalet les Mélèzes. If the cheque had come a day sooner, they might have mistaken God's leading and bought Sapins then. With Hindu teachings taking place nearby, the L'Abri Praying Family persevered in prayer with greater fervency. And some who were drawn first to Sapins found Christ as Saviour at L'Abri. They prayed for twelve years to buy Chalet les Sapins, but were not allowed to until *after* the woman who bought it was 'hopefully converted' as she lay dying and Edith spoke to her *once again* about Jesus Christ, the Saviour. God will sometimes delay an answer to prayer so that someone else can be converted, and meet our needs in other ways in the interim.

Prayer

Dear Father, please keep me from getting discouraged, if others accuse me of lack of faith when I pray and the results seem delayed. Teach me why You delay in answering sometimes, so that I can teach others about Your faithfulness and love. Amen.

25

PRAYER AND HARD WORK

When he saw the crowds, he had compassion on them, because they were harassed and helpless, like sheep without a shepherd. Then he said to his disciples, 'The harvest is plentiful but the workers are few. Ask the Lord of the harvest, therefore, to send out workers into his harvest field.'

Matthew 9:36–38

When the Schaeffers founded L'Abri, they resolved they would not advertise for workers, but pray for the Lord of the harvest to send the people of His choice into the work. L'Abri still follows this policy, so each worker is looked upon as a special gift that God has sent into the work in answer to prayer. L'Abri workers do not serve the personal needs of the leaders, because everyone labours together in whatever work God wants them to do to help others. And the Schaeffers kept L'Abri from becoming a cult by resolving not to try to 'hang on' to any workers or members when they felt God was leading them away from the work.

L'Abri does not manipulate people, or say, as some of the cults do, 'If you walk away from us, you are walking away from God and His will for your life.' Whenever people leave L'Abri, they are blessed, commended and prayed for, so they can do God's work wherever He leads. Edith wrote what every Christian worker needs to understand in principle: 'There really is no difference in the total need; the field is the world and *place* to *be* is the place where *the Lord wants you*, and us, no other.'[1]

L'Abri workers have come from many countries: England, Germany, Japan, South Africa, Switzerland and the United States, to name only a few. Some were not 'official' workers, but were next-door neighbours who became Christians through L'Abri and volunteered their time as much as possible. Some left the opera to become workers and stay in L'Abri, and some left L'Abri to be pastors and professors and take a L'Abri understanding into their churches, colleges and seminaries.

Since L'Abri workers have come from nearly every profession and trade, they have learned how the Christian faith applies to every area of life. Therefore, God has uniquely gifted and guided L'Abri to meet the needs of each seeker God sends at any time from any place. By seeking the Lord's leading and asking Him to place the people and workers of His choice where He wants them, L'Abri's teachings have spread throughout the world and into businesses, churches, governments, hospitals and schools.

In French, L'Abri literally means 'shelter', and it is a spiritual shelter for many who come. In English, for its helpers, workers and members, L'Abri has come to mean 'Slogging': for them, L'Abri means 'working hard and toiling' to meet the needs of others whatever they may be. One cannot emphasise too strongly that those who help in L'Abri *work hard, long hours* so that they can care for those who have spiritual needs. Giving honest answers to honest questions requires long hours of study in many fields in addition to the study of the Bible and theology. Listening for a better understanding of a person to know his real needs and how to meet them requires patience hour after hour. Answering complex questions individually or in groups requires meeting a variety of needs all at once. Many in L'Abri call this 'slogging'. If a person does not believe he is called by God into the work of L'Abri, he will not work this hard.

L'Abri workers do more than just think hard and talk. They clean chicken houses, shovel manure, chop wood, repair plumbing, cook meals for large numbers of people, visit hospitals and churches, and supervise students in their work and studies. L'Abri means praying for money to buy food, but also ploughing, planting, hoeing and reaping from large gardens. To feed hungry guests and workers in 1961, Swiss L'Abri planted forty-five different types of seeds: of beans, beets, broccoli, cabbage, cauliflower, celery, corn, cucumbers, lettuce, peas, spinach, radishes and turnips. No wonder when Edith joined others and prayed one January, 'Oh, Lord, if it be Thy will that we put aside some of this crop for winter use, please send us a freezer by the time the peas are full in the pods,' the Lord answered on the very day she requested.[2] The labour in L'Abri can be truly appreciated only by those who have taken part in the work.

In a real sense, those in L'Abri have *more than earned* the gifts that people send in answer to their prayers for the needy. God's way of 'paying' them is an untraditional way of sending money and gifts from various people when needed in answer to prayer. And God has never sent gifts so that anyone in L'Abri could have a life of leisure or luxury. Sometimes the need has been so great that when someone has found a half-used tube of toothpaste left by a guest, they have rejoiced at God's provision.

The Schaeffers and others in L'Abri work hard for God, as hard as many labour for an earthly employer or material gain. Living by faith as a means of leisure tempts God and indicates a mistaken attitude towards work and not worrying about our life. The temptation to use prayer as the easy way out of things is so great that we need to pray for God to help us stay right with Him through the cleansing blood of Jesus Christ. Having faith that God will hear us when we pray is often built up by working hard in His harvest field, rather than seeking ways to avoid hard work and responsibility. To give up our job and decide to live by faith alone for material provisions does not mean giving up hard work, and must be a step of faith based upon the Scriptures and how God has providentially prepared and led us in the past.

Those in secular work are living by faith when they pray for God to lead them in giving their financial and prayer support to those in Christian work. They are living by faith when they pray for God to help them represent Him truly to their bosses and co-workers as they try to be good examples and witnesses. God calls us to pray and follow Him, to prepare and go, to obey and work hard and give Him all the glory for taking care of us each day. And then in times of trouble and uncertainty, in times of looking for a job or a place to live and food to eat, we can call out to God and remember the Bible's promise: 'He will respond to the prayer of the destitute; he will not despise their plea' (Psalm 102:17).

When God is first in our lives and Jesus is our only Master, we can live and pray and trust in His promise to care for all our needs, even as He cares for the birds of the air. As those in L'Abri worked hard each day, they did face destitution at times, but God always provided. On 24 August, 1965, Edith looked back over ten years of L'Abri and wrote:

> We repeatedly have discovered through ten years of living in this realm, by prayer, that one *must* go through dark periods of real testing, of 'low times' and 'dark moments', facing real need, going through times of enforced frugality and deprivation (not pretend ones!), in order to see the reality of answered prayer; in order to know that the money is not coming in in an easily explained 'expected' way, but is truly a miracle of answered prayer.[3]

Prayer

Dear Heavenly Father, help me count the cost of service before I put my hand to the plough. Help me to look ahead as I work, so I will not look back with regret. Help me know Your will for me, and then give me the courage to step out in faith and follow You. Give me the strength to work the long hard hours that may be needed, not just to meet my needs, but to also help those who must have their spiritual and physical needs met by me as they trust in You alone for help. In Jesus' name. Amen.

—— 26 ——————————————

PRAYER AND SACRIFICE

And we pray this in order that you may live a life worthy of the Lord and may please him in every way: bearing fruit in every good work, growing in the knowledge of God . . . And pray for us, too, that God may open a door for our message, so that we may proclaim the mystery of Christ, for which I am in chains. Pray that I may proclaim it clearly, as I should.

Colossians 1:10; 4:3–4

After Jesus Christ met Paul on the road to Damascus and led him to salvation, he was overjoyed. He knew he was not worthy to be saved, because he had persecuted Christians; therefore, he never ceased praising God for His grace. And Jesus Christ made such a difference in his life that he began telling others that Jesus could do the same for them. As the years passed, he was overwhelmed more and more each time he thought about all that Jesus Christ had sacrificed so that he and others might be saved from sin and hell. And just like his Saviour, he joyfully began sacrificing all the comforts of this world to preach the gospel—even being flogged and imprisoned if necessary. He seldom thought of what he was sacrificing for others, because he kept his focus on all that God had sacrificed for him through His Son.

Saving faith supernaturally leads us to a willingness to sacrifice for others, as God and others have sacrificed for us. Those who went to L'Abri saw daily how much the Schaeffers and all the helpers and workers sacrificed so that they could learn the truth and be given good reasons to accept Jesus as the Messiah. And when they came to faith, the Holy Spirit filled them with such joy in believing that they naturally wanted others to know that same joy through Christ. They knew the peace and joy of living in God's Kingdom *now* by experience, and wanted others to know the same things: 'For the kingdom of God is not a matter of eating and drinking, but of *righteousness, peace and joy in the Holy Spirit*, because anyone who serves Christ in this way is pleasing to God and approved by men' (Romans 14:17–18, emphasis mine). Once they entered into a supernatural way of living, they began to act on the basis of the character of Jesus Christ, which He was forming within them. Sacrifice became a natural thing, rather than a burden to bear with resentment.

L'Abri has helped thousands of people become Christians, because many of those who were saved at L'Abri went out and led others to saving faith with the same spirit of sacrifice as they saw at L'Abri. They did not go out with a legalistic resolution, saying something like, 'They sacrificed for me, now I *have to* sacrifice too.' No. The Spirit of Jesus Christ filled them with His love and joy, so the love of Jesus spurred them into action—to do all they could to lead others to the Saviour no matter what the cost.

They acted on the basis of what they saw modelled around them, and saw how reasonable and right it was to sacrifice to promote the well-being and eternal happiness of others. God led them to the place of looking for ways to bless others, and the cost in time, energy or material things became secondary to serving God and others—meeting *real* needs. They did not sacrifice 'to be saved', or 'to earn points with God', or 'to obligate God when they prayed'. They sacrificed because the Holy Spirit supernaturally leads those who are saved to make sacrifices out of a heart full of love for God and others. And after we have sacrificed and done all we can for God, our spirit still says in our hearts: 'We are unworthy servants; we have only done our duty' (Luke 17:10).

The Schaeffers never asked anyone to sacrifice for the work of L'Abri, but the Lord sometimes led those who were saved through L'Abri to sacrifice that the gospel might be spread. After Jane Stuart Smith gave her life to the Lord, she also gave God her exquisite and expensive opera costumes. And when people began to pray for money to build a chapel at L'Abri, Jane began to pray that the Lord would send an opera singer her size, who also sang her various parts in opera, who could buy her costumes so she could give to the chapel fund. It seemed an impossible situation, but the Lord honoured her desire to sacrifice for His glory and promote the salvation and happiness of others by sending her a woman from Yugoslavia who could wear all of her clothes, who sang all of her parts, and who rejoiced at finding such beautiful costumes that she could afford to buy.

When the bee keeper, who lived near Chalet

les Mélèzes and who had become a Christian under the Schaeffers' ministry, learned that L'Abri could not afford to build a chapel, he volunteered to dig the foundation. And his leadership influenced others in L'Abri to volunteer their labour to build the chapel themselves. As he led in prayer for God's protection of the workers each day and for good weather to get the roof finished on time, his prayerful sacrifice was noted by some of those living in the village, and they reported that they had never seen such a mild December and January while workers were on the roof.

Some young people have prayed for and sacrificially given their savings to send a friend, a brother, or sister to L'Abri, because 'they so need to hear these truths too'. Others have postponed trips or used a part of their salaries to send money to buy more property 'for more room', or to buy more food, or beds or tape recorders for students, or to support a student friend at L'Abri. No one at L'Abri asked anyone to make these sacrifices. Each person has sacrificed because God has moved them in answer to their prayers or the prayers of others. No one pressures anyone to give to L'Abri. The L'Abri Family Letters report some of the needs and have requested prayers, but there has never been enough space in the letters to tell about *all* the needs. And God has met every need, those spoken and unspoken, by His grace through prayer to build up people's faith and meet real needs.

Jesus loved and sacrificed for His enemies. We need to ask God to give us the same love for the worldly-minded that Jesus Christ has. Only if we have the mind of Christ will we be willing to sacrifice for them and supernaturally be able to show them the love Jesus Christ has for them.

One great difficulty for Christians is spending enough time in prayer to develop the love of Jesus for those who are His enemies and ours. How much are we willing to sacrifice that Jesus Christ may be honoured and His enemies come to saving faith—not to mention our loved ones and friends? Wouldn't we be more effective in prayer, if we prayed for Christ's sacrificial spirit to rule in our lives throughout the day? Edith Schaeffer wrote to the L'Abri Family: 'Oh, what a work there *could* be in homes scattered through the world, if the Holy Spirit would be given His place in the lives of Christians unhindered by the terrible demands self makes when 'self' takes first place in hearts!'[1] To pray effectively, we must have a spirit of sacrifice. And much true prayer will lead us to sacrifice. Our prayers for unbelievers, confused believers, and others need to flow supernaturally from hearts remade in the image of Jesus Christ, who died that we might live.

Prayer

Dear Heavenly Father, give me the sacrificial love of Your Son for others. He died that rebels in Your Kingdom might be saved. Give me the love of Jesus: not to meet any selfish desire to feel good, but to motivate and empower me to seek and save the lost as effectively as He did. Help me to be more willing to make any necessary sacrifices to promote Your cause upon this earth, that You might receive the honour You deserve. Amen.

— 27 —————————

PRAYER AND GROWTH

> *They devoted themselves to the apostles' teaching and to the fellowship, to the breaking of bread and to prayer.*
>
> **Acts 2:42**

When the Schaeffer family began L'Abri, they were perfectly willing for it always to be a small work, of only two or three people at a time asking questions, *if that were God's will for them.* They did not succumb to the world's notion that success means material growth, larger buildings or more people in one's organisation. Nor did they pray for that type of success. They prayed only for the people of the Lord's choice to come to their home and for His provision to meet their needs. They did not pray for large or small numbers, but only for God to send any needy people that He had prepared to serve in their House of Prayer. They did not specify the type of people for God to send, but they did want to do the work of evangelism.

Because they wanted to lead sinners to the Saviour, God often sent them people whose lifestyle and thoughts were radically opposed to their own; people who were often desperate because they had come to see the futility of their beliefs and ways of living. Therefore, to demonstrate His ability to answer prayer and because His compassion for these types of people is so great, God very quickly sent them as many as seventy-five people at a time to eat and ask questions in their small living room in Chalet les Mélèzes.

The sudden and unexpected growth in numbers at L'Abri meant the Schaeffers immediately needed to begin praying for more space, food and beds for all those coming to their home. And as the work grew, they needed to pray for more and different material things; for books, tapes and tape recorders for those who came to study. Some who had been saved before they founded L'Abri helped when they could, but they needed to begin praying immediately for full-time helpers, because those with needs far surpassed their physical capabilities and strength.

God had prepared Fran, Edith and the girls for a larger work when they began L'Abri, but because the needs were so great, the larger work meant they needed to pray harder and longer and eventually remain constantly in prayer. For the Schaeffers, prayer became a state of mind and not just words. Prayer became a constant concern of their loving heart for others. Just as a mother with a critically ill child will think about her child day and night until her concern becomes a permanent state of mind and the child is saved or dies, prayer for the Schaeffers became a state of constant intercession.

God led the Schaeffers into a prayerful state of mind for the many who came with desperate spiritual needs, and God never lifted that prayerful state, partly because they love God so much and partly because the needs of others are so great. At times the needs of those who came were so complex and beyond them, that the words of Paul took on greater meaning as they prayed, wept and sighed before the Lord: 'In the same way, the Spirit helps us in our weakness. We do not know what we ought to pray for, but the Spirit himself intercedes for us with groans that words cannot express' (Romans 8:26).

Prayer for God to bless our labours does involve *our* willingness always to be a 'small work', if that is God's will for us. Size is no measure of success, but we are not to use our willingness to be small as an excuse to be lazy. The Schaeffers had determined to work hard for God, even if the fruit would always be small. Attracting large crowds is no measure of our faithfulness to God—many large groups of people have been gathered together for less than noble causes: the large adoring crowds Adolf Hitler attracted before and after he began World War II are a case in point. Only a warped view of success would consider Hitler successful.

Success is not measured by size, but by faithfulness. Are we doing all that we know God wants us to do at this present moment? That is faithfulness. Are we praying for God to do His work in us, and use us, any way that He wants to? That is faithfulness. God will bring about the growth that He wants to achieve through us. The fruit of our labours for Him depends on Him.

To discover some of the key elements in faithfulness and the fruit God wants us to bear, we need to see what the book of Acts reveals regarding the results of the apostles' faithful preaching and teaching: those who were saved *devoted themselves to the apostles' teaching and to the*

fellowship, to the breaking of bread and to prayer.
L'Abri was faithful in modelling the practice of the
New Testament Church, though L'Abri is a
fellowship and not a church or congregation.
Those in L'Abri devoted themselves 'to the
apostles' teaching'; that is, they devoted
themselves to the Scriptures—to hearing and
obeying the Word of God. Devotion means serving
or obeying with a heartfelt concern, a loyal and
deep affection. 'Doing our devotions' has come to
mean a brief moment of prayer and Bible reading
each day, but some may try to substitute that for
serving the Lord with devotion and deep affection.
No matter how small L'Abri remained or how
large it grew, devotion to the apostles' teaching
would be used by God as a measure of its success,
and that is how God measures any work for Him.

God expects His people to be concerned about
fellowship, and the L'Abri schedule gave plenty of
time for fellowship around the 'breaking of bread'
(mealtimes), as well as while working in gardens
or kitchens. Many who came to L'Abri had never
experienced Christian fellowship before. They had
never experienced the love and care of a family
until they became a part of the L'Abri family. An
essential part of the Schaeffers meeting the needs
of those who came meant being a family for them,
and helping them find or begin a fellowship or

'family' when they left L'Abri. It meant remembering those in prayer who had come and gone from L'Abri.

The New Testament Church devoted herself to prayer, to spending real time with God: people together praying to and praising God. Prayer has always been primary in L'Abri, but not the only thing those in L'Abri do. Rather, they immerse everything they do in prayer, and God empowers their work in answer to prayer.

All of these elements of the New Testament Church will supernaturally flow from people who have come to love the Lord and each other because they truly appreciate God and each other. They will be of one mind and heart, not because order has been imposed from without or threats are made by the group's leaders, but because the Holy Spirit has given them unity through a common faith. Their unity of faith and love makes their prayers more effective and they can accomplish greater things for God.

L'Abri grew as God gave the growth, but L'Abri's growth is not measure of its faithfulness to God. However, we can praise God that by His grace those in L'Abri are faithful to God and the Scriptures, to the great evangelical commission, to the fellowship of true believers and to meeting the needs of others materially and spiritually by prayer.

Prayer

Dear Heavenly Father, thank You for making L'Abri grow. Thank You for sending people who need help. Thank You for the gift of workers, and for their gift of strength and character to help those You send to L'Abri. Give me Your perspective on life and success as I read Your Word. Keep me from being misled by the worldly-minded and the world's ideas of success. Keep me faithful to You and Your Son always. Amen.

— 28 —

ASKING GREAT THINGS FROM GOD

> *You, my God, have revealed to your servant that you will build a house for him. So your servant has found courage to pray to you.*
>
> 1 Chronicles 17:25

We must be careful not to measure our success by our size, but we need to remember that God is honoured by the size of our requests. We need to ask great things from God, not for selfish reasons,

237

but to serve Him and others better. We need to ask great things, expect great things and attempt great things to glorify and honour God.

As L'Abri began and grew, Fran and Edith began to ask for greater and greater blessings from God. God led them to pray for a $1,000 down payment to buy their first chalet, Chalet les Mélèzes, so that they could stay in Switzerland. And then He taught them to pray for the next step, a second, larger payment to close their purchase.

After a few years, when God showed them the great need for more effective evangelism and missionary efforts, He taught them to pray for thousands of dollars for more homes, more workers and more L'Abri fellowships wherever He wanted them. He led them to write their first books to help people with some basic problems, and then they discovered He wanted them to write about how He is Lord over the whole of life, and this required a whole series of books. To reach even greater numbers, He led them to do the film series and books *How Should We Then Live?* and *Whatever Happened to the Human Race?*[1] And then after Dr Schaeffer discovered he had cancer in 1978, God empowered Him to write more books about Christ's lordship over human governments and evangelical churches.[2]

Fran and Edith Schaeffer did not begin L'Abri

in 1955 by asking God for all these great things, or by asking Him to make them into very important people. After they resolved to follow Him, they simply prayed for God to unfold His plan for their lives. And each year God taught them to pray for greater things until they began reaching many thousands of people through their books and films in places where L'Abri could not go.[3] When we read Edith's letters home, we see that those in L'Abri were constantly expecting great things from God, and God never failed them. But with every prayer by every member, God seemed to stretch them beyond human endurance and intelligence so the work would be truly His work within them and not theirs alone.

God considers it an honour when we ask great things from Him in order to bless more and more people, and He is glorified more and more when He honours these requests. God does not expect us to pray for great things all at once without His leading. He will build our faith by leading us day by day to pray with greater expectations; expectations based upon what He has done with us in the past. Francis and Edith Schaeffer did not pray for greater things for themselves, but always for God to be glorified and more people to be blessed by coming to know the truth. Because they prayed from a heartfelt love for God and others, He could honour their prayers.

As the Schaeffers and others in L'Abri prayed, they also expected and attempted greater things of themselves. The work grew when Fran began travelling to teach the Bible and answer questions rather than stay at home: people who had been saved in their home wanted their friends to hear Fran's teaching. And then the work grew larger when people wanted to come to L'Abri as students—not just guests or helpers—but to study, daily and deeply, the Scriptures and what Fran was teaching about Christianity and culture. Since they had prayed for God's plan and for God to give the growth, they believed these requests were a part of God's plan and they began Farel House for students.

Farel House has grown to be a part of each L'Abri branch, because God showed them that it was worthy of their labours and His blessings.[4] As they prayed for greater and greater things, they also paid the price for these greater things. Writing books and making films required more hours of work than they had ever done before in L'Abri or with Farel House students, and they had to do these greater things while continuing their work in L'Abri and with students.

Praying for greater things required them to work hard, learning new things daily to keep up with all that God was requiring them to do in answer to their prayers. God did greater and greater things for them in answer to their prayers, but each of these things required more of them. God continued to bless them and others with these greater ministries because they never used God or prayed for greater things so they could do less and less. So, we can see even more clearly why Edith might ask someone who says they want a prayer life like hers, 'Are you willing to pay the price of asking great things of God?'

In religious circles, some have taught that anyone can do whatever he really desires; that all of our desires are given by God and God would not give us a desire that we could not fulfil. A little common sense would dispel this notion. Some people no taller than four feet six inches have strongly desired to play professional basketball, but no matter how hard they have worked they have not succeeded. We would do better to teach that if we *strongly want God's desires* (plans and purposes) for our lives, and if we are *willing to follow His desires* whatever they may be, then *God will show us His desires and empower us* to fulfil them. We should also emphasise that many times God will only show us the next small step, and that we must take the next small step before He will show us His larger plan. Remember, God revealed

His plan for L'Abri one day at a time as they prayed.

Rather than teaching that God will fulfil our every desire, we should say that God will fulfil His every promise. David prayed with the faith that God would keep His promise to him and build him a house, and this gave him courage to pray and ask God to keep His promise (1 Chronicles 17:25). But David was also willing to do whatever God required of him to build his house. He did not sit back expecting God to do all while he did nothing. David knew that building his house would be a joint project between God and himself, and that his house would remain strong from generation to generation depending upon the faithfulness and obedience of his descendants—for God was always faithful. God would keep His promises to David, but would David and his descendants fulfil their part? History shows God remained faithful, but many of David's descendants had to be punished for their sins.

We need to rejoice and think about how much God strongly desires to *work with us*. God enjoys working with His children to accomplish great things. God finds true happiness when His children come to Him and ask Him if they can do something with Him and for Him, and God loves doing all that He wisely can with His children. Our Heavenly Father really does desire to do worthwhile things with each of us. And because He is infinite, He has all the time we need to work with Him. Perhaps the greatest thing we ever do is bring God true happiness by asking to be with Him and work with Him to accomplish His plans.

Prayer

Dear Heavenly Father, thank You for being a real Father to me. Thank You for truly desiring to spend time with me when You have the entire universe to care for. Thank You for stooping down to work with me and teach me what I need to know to help others. Help me treat others, especially my own family, the way You treat me. In Jesus' name and for His family. Amen.

29

OUR WORK OR GOD'S WORK

> 'Naked I came from my mother's womb, and naked I shall depart. The LORD gave and the LORD has taken away; may the name of the LORD be praised.' In all this, Job did not sin by charging God with wrongdoing.
>
> Job 1: 21–22

We honour God with the size of our requests, and God considers Himself honoured when we request great things from Him. Through the psalmist God promises, 'Open wide your mouth and I will fill it,' but that does not mean we should ask for selfish things or things unworthy of Him or ourselves. God promises that by His grace He will give us all that we need to honour Him in an unbelieving world; therefore, He encourages us to open wide our mouths so He can fill us with all we need to glorify Him.

If we reduced the size of our requests for God's blessings because of our unworthiness, our requests would always be smaller than they should be. In the name of Jesus Christ, we should ask God for great things because He is great in mercy; He has made great promises to His children; and His heart is so full of love that He longs to pour out great blessings upon us. And yet, if we are practising sin, God first commands us to repent and ask for His forgiveness through His Son before we ask for other things.

If we love our Saviour, we will endeavour to live a righteous life in Him so that God can work in us. Jesus is our great Advocate, and He intercedes for us according to our needs and does great things in us to honour His Heavenly Father. Because God saved us through His Son, He encourages us to come to Him with any request that is worthy of His name, whether large or small.

God can use us, anyone or anything, as a tool; much as we would use a hammer or saw to build a house. God used Moses and Pharaoh, but in radically different ways. God used Moses as His friend, and taught him to pray and ask great things of Him to bless His people. God used Pharaoh as an enemy, and brought glory to Himself in spite of Pharaoh's hard heart. We need to ask ourselves how we want to be used.

Francis and Edith Schaeffer asked God to use them as His friends, and use them in any way He pleased to lead others to saving faith in Jesus Christ. God delighted to hear their prayers for money to build a chapel or to make a film series so that they could spread His Word. God granted them great things, because they wanted great things to promote His cause; and when God gave them great things, they praised Him and gave Him all the glory for His marvellous grace in Christ Jesus. As His friends, God taught them to rely on His faithfulness, His promises, His love and His grace in Jesus Christ, and as they relied upon Him they received blessing after blessing.

Perhaps most of all, from what God taught the Schaeffers about prayer, we need to learn that we will honour God the most when we allow His character to shine forth from our lives. God will not duplicate a L'Abri for every Christian who asks to have that type of ministry in their home. God will not make every Christian into a 'Christian celebrity' or give everyone who asks for it a television, radio or writing ministry. But God will give every Christian the grace to reveal His character to those around them. In many religious and nonreligious circles today, to be called 'pious' is derogatory, but to be pious means to show a sense of duty and loyalty to God, to our parents, to our friends, to our employers and employees, and to others who have a claim upon us. All Christians need to be pious in this sense.

If we ask Jesus Christ to change our character, attitude and disposition, and manifest His true devotion and loyalty to God through us, then we will bring more honour to God than those who have or have had a 'celebrity ministry' without the Christian character to back it up. All Christians can honour God by bringing forth the fruits of the Holy Spirit. And others will be drawn to Christ as Saviour as we pray for the Holy Spirit to bear His fruit in our lives, because many unbelievers have become cynical through their disappointment in 'celebrity ministries':

But the fruit of the Spirit is love, joy, peace, patience, kindness, goodness, faithfulness, gentleness and self-control. Against such things there is no law. Those who belong to Christ Jesus have crucified the sinful nature [flesh] with its passions and desires. Since we live by the Spirit, let us keep in step with the Spirit. Let us not become conceited, provoking and envying each other (Galatians 5:22–26).

We can become a friend of God, as Moses was, and be used by God as His friend, by walking in the Spirit instead of fulfilling our desires in forbidden ways. As we pray daily for God's grace and friendship, He will be with us in the good times as well as the bad, and we will be open to receive His sustaining grace.

Consider Job. As a friend of God, he honoured God more than anyone else of his generation. God said of him, 'There is no one on earth like him; he is blameless and upright, a man who fears God and shuns evil' (Job 1:8). And yet, in the spiritual battle, all the great things Job had were taken away from him: his children, his home, his wealth, his health and the helpful support of his wife and friends. Job felt as though he had been abandoned by God and stripped completely naked; and yet, by the grace of God he remained faithful to God and sinned not. He had to admit his ignorance before God, but in the spiritual battle he did not rebel against God.

God used Job in a way that manifested His righteous character in him, and told Job's friends that if they asked Job, he would pray for them and bless them. If everything external is taken from us, or if our health fails, through prayer we will glorify God and maintain our Christian character in spite of everything.

If God so blesses us, and gives us a work that attracts the attention of others, God may allow us to be tested in special ways to bring Him honour. Through this testing, we can show others that *we truly believe* that whatever we have achieved is really God's work or achievement and not ours. This testing may be like Job's, when everything is taken from us. If we lose our ministry (not because we have sinned against God and man), or if our church burns, will we tell others how much loss *we* have suffered, or will we grieve and consider how much *God* has lost or suffered? If we have believed the work or ministry or chapel was really His and not ours, we will grieve because of the loss to God and the possible setback this may be in the work of leading many to salvation, and begin to pray for Him to be glorified and Satan defeated so many will still be saved. Sometimes we can be tested by the loss of things so that we can glorify God and manifest His character and sustaining grace in these dark times.

As the Schaeffers were successfully showing *How Should We Then Live?* in seminars across America, they received one blow after another. Among their afflictions, Edith's father died, their new chapel burned, and its beautiful organ was damaged. In this affliction and loss, they passed the test and glorified God: they did not charge God with wrongdoing. The Lord had given and the Lord had taken away by allowing Satan to test them, and then the Lord overruled all for their good and manifested His love.

Prayer

Dear Heavenly Father, I pray that Jesus Christ and His character will shine forth from my life regardless of my circumstances or afflictions. Inspire me to ask great things and expect great things from You for Jesus' sake. Amen.

30

JESUS' PRAYER AND GOD'S WORK IN US

I have given them your word and the world has hated them, for they are not of the world any more than I am of the world. My prayer is not that you take them out of the world but that you protect them from the evil one. They are not of the world, even as I am not of it. Sanctify them by the truth; your word is truth. As you sent me into the world, I have sent them into the world.

John 17:14–18

*I*nstead of leading us to withdraw from the world, a life of prayerful obedience will lead us to confront an unbelieving world and a rebellious church with the exclusive claims of Jesus Christ. We will pray for the Lord over all to give us wisdom to understand the world spirit of our age, so we can oppose error by rightly applying God's truth to its points of deception and weakness. We will pray for Jesus Christ to give us the ability to wage spiritual warfare in the heavenly realms against the principalities and powers of the air. And we will ask Him to give us the courage and strength to speak and write the truth persuasively—to increase the size of God's army and defeat the forces of darkness that are deceiving humankind.

Beginning in the early 1970s, God opened the door for Francis and Edith Schaeffer to have a greater public ministry, but not in the sense that we have been accustomed to expect. They did not become celebrities, but began to speak out against the evils that were spreading into every area of government, society, culture and the church.

Because Jesus Christ prayed for them before He died, as He has prayed for all true believers, and because He continued to intercede for them in heaven, He sent them into the world as He had been sent. And the world mistreated them as it mistreated Jesus Christ almost 2,000 years ago.

As we review their ministry, we see first that Jesus led them to fight His battles against a theology in the churches that denied the infallibility of the Scriptures and the deity of Christ. Then He led them to fight the humanism and rationalism that dominates governments, educational establishments and the media. Because reform movements always spring from true revival, they worked to unite biblical Christians to reform the church, government and society. And just as the revivals in America in the early 1800s motivated Christians to work for the abolition of slavery, so the revival that continued in and spread beyond L'Abri motivated the Schaeffers and others to fight against abortion, infanticide, 'mercy killing', and other social injustices. Almost all the credit for uniting Protestant Christians to oppose abortion must be given to the leadership Jesus Christ inspired the Schaeffers to give through L'Abri.

In 1976, when they began attacking humanism with *How Should We Then Live?*, Satan intensified his attacks against L'Abri; their chapel burned and other tragedies happened. Many in L'Abri and those who supported them experienced attacks against property and people similar to those at the beginning of L'Abri in 1955. But this time, the attacks would not subside until Fran died of cancer in 1984.

The more they prayed and obeyed, the more intense the spiritual battle became, but Jesus had prepared them so Fran could fight this final battle. Notice how Jesus Christ answered His own prayer in John 17 in their behalf. First, He gave them His Word and taught them that the Bible was absolutely true in every area that it addressed, especially in the historical, moral and spiritual realms. He taught them by experience and study that He could be absolutely trusted in everything.

Second, by His truth and Spirit, He led them to sanctify, consecrate or set themselves apart to obey Him in all things and teach others to do the same. We have seen how they resolved to live so close to the Lord that they would recognise and obey His will through the Scriptures, His promises, providence and the Holy Spirit—in any way that Jesus chose to reveal His will for them.

Third, Jesus protected them from the evil one as they followed His plan. He did not keep them from suffering all of Satan's assaults, either mentally, physically or spiritually; but He protected them from being overcome and defeated by Satan. He protected them from Satan's deceitfulness and doing anything that would disgrace God's cause or themselves—and perhaps this is the most important form of protection that

Jesus Christ can give any of us in this life. As Christians grow in their faith, they will often suffer in ways that Jesus Christ suffered Himself, and by His grace they will not deny or disgrace Him, even as He remained faithful under trial until death.

Dr Schaeffer did not begin his last battles in the best of health. He began his public battle against abortion, infanticide and euthanasia by making his last film series, *Whatever Happened to the Human Race?* at the age of 66, and as he was fighting lymphoma in its advancing stages (though he did not know this until a few days after he had filmed his last episode). After his book and film were in final form and while he was undergoing chemotherapy, he lectured and answered questions on Christianity and medical ethics at seminars in America, England and other parts of Europe. Because some doctors told him in 1978 that he had only six weeks to six months to live, he prayed and fought hard to speak the truth while he still had time. He prayed that God would give him daily strength to fight and heal him through his medical treatments. In answer to his prayers, and the prayers of thousands, God gave him the strength to go on, and he spoke on the major issues of our time to some at the White House in America and to some members of Parliament in England.

The battle against abortion led him to look closely at the role of Christians and the government, and the Holy Spirit inspired him to write *The Christian Manifesto* to motivate Christians to work for reform in government. Then finally his attention turned back to the Church; this time the evangelical church. He grieved over many evangelical church leaders accepting a low view of the authority of Scripture and then relaxing biblical moral standards for themselves and others in the Church. He spoke out strongly in his last book, *The Great Evangelical Disaster*, and then completed another series of seminars one month before he died from lymphoma on 15 May, 1984, in Rochester, Minnesota.

Christians seldom have the luxury of fighting only one battle at a time. Only through prayer and obedience will we discover the battles we must fight, learn how to fight them, and be given the strength to do the will of God no matter what the personal cost. If anything, perhaps the Schaeffers gave the greatest demonstration of God's power and the reality of answered prayer *after* Dr Schaeffer discovered he had cancer. While receiving treatment, he lived more than five years, wrote three new books, completely revised his complete works, lectured around the world, and fought the biggest battles of our time in the Church, government and society. In every case, he rallied others to carry on the battle, so after he died many in our churches and those inside and outside government have made great reforms, though we still have much to do before Jesus Christ returns.

Prayer

Dear Father, whenever I am tempted to give up because my troubles are so great or things seem hopeless, remind me that with You all things are possible. Keep me faithful. Amen.

—— 31 ————————————

LIFE AFTER DEATH

Therefore let everyone who is godly pray to you while you may be found; surely when the mighty waters rise, they will not reach him.

Psalm 32:6

As I write this last meditation, Edith Schaeffer is 78 years old and still working hard, spending most of her time in Rochester L'Abri. God willing, she will be 79 on 3 November, 1993. Almost nine years have passed since the death of her husband, and she has carried on their work with the talents and tireless energy God gives her. The mighty waters often rose as they fought together, especially in Fran's last years, but they continued in prayer and God sustained her faith through Fran's illness and after his death. Over more than thirty years, the Schaeffers and L'Abri have demonstrated God's power through prayer to overcome Satan in all things and glorify God.

By His Spirit, God often gives widows, or widowers, more opportunities to serve Him, and demonstrates His power to overcome their tragic loss and bring good out of evil. He will heal us with His love, and enable us to glorify Him and disappoint Satan by empowering us to go on because Jesus Christ has defeated our last enemy—death.

> 'Death has been swallowed up in victory. '
> 'Where, O death, is your victory? Where, O death, is your sting?' The sting of death is sin, and the power of sin is the law. But thanks be to God! He gives us the victory through our Lord Jesus Christ. Therefore, my dear brothers, stand firm. Let nothing move you. Always give yourselves fully to the work of the Lord, because you know that your labour in the Lord is not in vain (1 Corinthians 15:54–58).

By His grace, God has given Edith Schaeffer a wider ministry as a widow than she knew when Fran was alive. To demonstrate the reality of prayer, and to show that God is all-sufficient to meet every need, God allowed Fran to die before Edith, and He has shown through her that He can accomplish great things through single individuals who are devoted to honouring Him.

After the death of Francis Schaeffer, Edith came forth from serving in the background with a new life and vitality all her own. Intellectually, she is equal to her husband, and still carries on discussions with believers and unbelievers in much the same way as he did. As a writer, she is more prolific than her husband, and all of her writings apply her husband's innovative approach to philosophical and theological teaching in the practical areas of home and family life. With her autobiographical works, she shows how they lived on the basis of their teachings and how God answered their prayers. When Fran and Edith were married, God blended two lives together in a beautiful way to serve Him; and apart, God has given her the guidance and strength to reach out successfully into new areas of ministry, such as the arts and music.[1]

Edith Schaeffer still prays for those of the Lord's choice to come to L'Abri and for the Lord to provide the food and shelter for those He sends.

As she prepares her menus for those coming to dinner, she still prays for God to send His 'surprise' guests. One of her delights is asking each person who knocks on her door, 'Well, how did you get here?' because she wants to learn how God has been working in their lives to bring them to L'Abri, that God might be glorified immediately for His leading. Some, who have misunderstood her question, have replied, 'Well, *you* invited me!'

Edith prays for those coming to L'Abri for high tea as she cooks, but she does not pray out of a legalistic compulsion, thinking, 'Now I am preparing a menu, so now I must take time to pray for people to come and eat.' No, she prays out of her love and wonder to a God who will send her people to serve. She prays for the specific needs of those she knows will be there, because she knows that her prayers will make a difference in each one who comes. She prays that their questions may be answered, or that they will ask questions that will help others, and that God will give her the needed answers to share. Prayer for others is the natural and supernatural joy of her life, because Jesus is her closest Friend and she maintains a Christlike, servant-spirit through Him. Her prayers for others come naturally, because God has implanted His love for us in her heart.

When people talk to Edith on the phone, almost always before they hang up, Edith says,

'Let's pray.' Whether a local or long-distance call, Edith prays. After almost 79 years, the life of prayer comes to her so spontaneously that silent and spoken prayers in almost every context make up a large part of her life in addition to her special daily quiet times.[2]

For her quiet times, Edith reads *Daily Light* each day, and in addition reads through her Bible. She does not skip around, but reads straight through expecting God to speak to her personally by His written Word. She writes notes or prayers to God in her Bible as she prays, and dates her notes. Over the years, she has written thousands of notes to God through several Bibles. She often prays in the context of a verse, using its words or phrases in praising God or in applying them to her spiritual needs, the needs of L'Abri or the needs of others.

When Edith prays out loud with others, she praises God and thanks Him especially for the work He has done through Christ in the person's life for whom she is praying. She thanks God for bringing the people of His choice together, and for the work He is now doing in each person's life. She intercedes for any special needs the other person has, and will pray for some of the needs of L'Abri, believing that when people unite in prayer God will respond as He has promised. These are some of the ways God has led the Edith to pray as

He has taught her over the years, and her prayer life is simply the supernatural outgrowth of her salvation and spiritual life.[3]

The ministry of L'Abri and Edith's continuing ministry is God's answer in the twentieth century to Paul's prayer in the first. Paul prayed for the Church: 'And this is my prayer: that your love may abound more and more in knowledge and depth of insight' (Philippians 1:9). A major purpose in life is loving God and others intelligently, and our prayer requests will reflect love, reason and faith as we pray and read the Bible. Indeed, as our knowledge and depth of insight increase, our love for God and compassion for others will increase. If not, we are not true believers or our orthodoxy has become cold and sterile.

Most of us have met some who have professed to be highly intelligent and Christian, who have allowed themselves to become puffed up with pride or who have used their intellect to beat down others or make others submit to their heartless doctrines. By the grace of God, Francis and Edith Schaeffer did not succumb to the temptation to use their intellect to build themselves up or tear others down. Through L'Abri, they remained humble servants of all, and their love for others motivated them to build others up in true faith; for this reason they led many sceptical and cynical people to the Saviour. By their example, they taught others to pray that increased knowledge would not puff them up, but show them more ways to express the love of God.

Prayer

Dear Father, as I go on in a life of prayer, and bring every need to You, strengthen me so I will not be anxious about anything. I will devote myself to prayer for Jesus' sake. Amen.

EPILOGUE

This is what the LORD says: 'Let not the wise man boast of his wisdom or the strong man boast of his strength or the rich man boast of his riches, but let him who boasts boast about this: that he understands and knows me, that I am the LORD, who exercises kindness, justice and righteousness on earth, for in these I delight,' declares the LORD.

Jeremiah 9:23–24

As I have read the biographies of great Christians, I have been more impressed by what God has taught them and done through them than by what they have done for God. I feel this way about Jonathan Edwards, John Wesley, Charles Finney, C. H. Spurgeon, Hudson Taylor, Andrew Murray and especially Francis and Edith Schaeffer. I firmly believe that God determined to prepare and call each of these leaders for their place in history before they were born, in order to bless thousands for generations. Before they were born, God prepared them physically and placed them where He could achieve His purposes. For example, C.

H. Spurgeon was physically prepared to preach to thousands without modern, electronic amplification. His photographic memory was God's gift, so he could preach and publish sermons that would move people even today, a hundred years after his death.

Francis Schaeffer was born to parents he had to lead to faith, and this helped him identify with nonbelievers. Edith Schaeffer was a child of faithful missionaries and born in China, and this helped her understand the special needs of those who had been raised in the Church but had problems with it. Through their opposite childhoods, God prepared them in a very special way to meet the needs of troubled young people from around the world. The Schaeffers could also function on very little sleep (Edith needed only about three hours a night), and this was essential for a work like L'Abri and all it led them to do.

If we measure our success and failures by the impact or size of great Christian leaders, we may always be disappointed. God has raised up leaders through the centuries to bless thousands and be a lasting example of faithfulness to succeeding generations. Jesus did not make every follower into an apostle, and we should not think that if we are less effective or less well known than other Christians in our day, that is a sign of our unfaithfulness or God's unfairness. God has a plan and purpose for each of us, and we need to follow Him whether that leads to places of greatness or small corners of the world.

No matter what role God wants us to take in His Kingdom, He will use enduring principles and similar procedures over and over again to teach people how to pray, to draw people close to Him, to transform their character into the image of Christ, to enable them to lead some to saving faith, and to empower them to bear fruit. We can learn these principles from Christian biography as well as theological books, but I have needed both to help me in my Christian walk.

In this book, I have carefully selected only a few answers to prayer in the Schaeffers' lives and in L'Abri, and these were selected to illustrate some spiritual principles and truths about prayer. I have not tried to write another biography on the Schaeffers, but I have tried to show how God led them prayer by prayer over the years and built their faith to teach them how to pray one day at a time. There did come a day when they had learned the major lessons God wanted to teach them, and then they needed to be faithful in prayer and teach others how to pray.

As we look over their lives, we find they received many blessings from God in answer to prayer, but as their prayers became more effective, God led them further into the spiritual battle and they were deeply wounded from time to time. A life of prayer may seem romantic, but if we enter into such a life with romantic reasons God will quickly show us the reality of a life of prayer, and we will need to make a decision about whether or not we intend to carry on or be sure that we are in the centre of God's will for us.

My presentation of the Schaeffers' prayer lives in this book may have seemed idealistic, but I have tried to dispel that notion as we have seen increased suffering along with greater answers to prayer. I have tried to show that God will teach us how to pray and be faithful, but that we can be faithful in works far different from L'Abri and that we should not try to duplicate anyone else's work unless we know with certainty that God wants us to model our ministry on someone else. When the Schaeffers modelled L'Abri on many of Hudson Taylor's prayer principles, they did not try to duplicate the China Inland Mission. We can model our lives on the prayer principles in this book, and be called to a new work for our time, just as Hudson Taylor and Francis Schaeffer were called to do a special work for their time.

Francis and Edith Schaeffer always strongly emphasised the importance of the choices we make and of our need to follow the Holy Spirit instead of doing our own thing. They were conscious every day of needing to make choices on how they would spend their time or where they would go or who they would talk to. And because they knew they were so limited, they prayed for the Holy Spirit to help them manage their lives with His daily guidance. They did not wait day after day for God to show them His total plan in some mystical way. They prayed and did all they could do for God each day, in ways they knew He would bless because they were scriptural, and then they discovered God's leading through their faithfulness to God in each day's tasks. When they had to make a big decision, such as whether or not to build a new building, they waited until God gave clear leading. But they did not stop serving Him daily in other ways while they waited for Him to show them when they could buy another chalet, for example. To have done that would have completely immobilised their ministry.

I do encourage you to study the appendices in this book. The first one will give you a good review of the book as a whole, and show you which chapter to turn to in order to find more information on any particular prayer principle. Perhaps you will discover some prayer principles in the appendix that you did not recognise as you read the book. The second appendix could help a church become a House of Prayer by studying and applying the principles in each chapter in small groups. A new prayer group could be formed by using the study guide or an older group could be renewed by praying together and learning some new principles. If you would like more information about L'Abri, I would encourage you to write, visit or call the L'Abri branch nearest you and you will find their addresses in Appendix III. For further reading and study of the Schaeffers' books, see the Endnotes.

If you have read this far, stop now and praise God for all that He has done for us through His Son, Jesus Christ, and thank Him for giving us the opportunity to have fellowship with Him and be His friend through prayer. Thank Him for all the Christians who have been faithful in prayer throughout the centuries, and pray that He will show you what He wants you to do with your life as you seek Him daily in prayer.

Prayer

Dear Father, I praise You for Your Son, Jesus Christ, and for His death for my sins. Help me turn from all sin and follow You faithfully. By Your Spirit, make me into the type of person You need to demonstrate Your character and reality. Place me where You want me to be so Your Kingdom may increase. Amen.

APPENDIX I

WHERE TO FIND SOME PRINCIPLES OF PRAYER

275

met. It also includes making promises to God and remaining faithful.

3. When we study the importance of making vows to the Lord, we learn another secret of power in prayer.

1. God's evident display of faithfulness should encourage us to pray and move ahead as He leads.

2. God knows what prayers to answer and when to answer them in order to have the greatest positive effect on the greatest number of people.

3. Only the Holy Spirit can give people an understanding heart, so we must make this a matter of prayer.

4. Living by faith and prayer alone takes a tremendous amount of work and requires great physical and spiritual strength.

1. We must pray for God to work in the spiritual realm and build our Christian character.

2. Only our living with consistency day by day will help many overcome their cynicism and scepticism about the validity of the Christian faith.

3. To have much power in prayer, we need to live holy lives, not in our own strength, but in a moment by moment dependence on the Holy Spirit.

20. *Hearing the Prayers of Unbelievers* 173
    (*Hebrews 11:6*)

1. When we love and bless our enemies our moral character is similar to the character of God and we are truly His children.

2. The way God's Son died as a human being demonstrated the extent of God's love for His enemies, and made the atonement the greatest event in human history.

3. Regarding prayer, we cannot say that God treats believers and unbelievers in exactly the same way.

4. The cries of the wicked are not the same as the prayers of the righteous, but God will sometimes hear the cries of the wicked. The Bible does not give the wicked any reason to believe that God will answer their prayers.

21. *Days of Fasting and Prayer*   181
(*Luke 5:35*)

1. Fasting indicates that we are willing to deny ourselves to follow Him.
2. Times of fasting and prayer are opportunities to draw near to God and prepare ourselves to receive Him when He draws near to us.
3. Fasting should indicate our absolute submission to the will of God.

22. *Confidence in Prayer and Our Conscience* 189
(*1 John 3:21–22*)

1. Times of fasting and prayer enable God to show us the true state of hearts: do we love God for who He is, or just for what He gives?
2. Jesus expects us to ask Him to fill us with the Holy Spirit so we are empowered to overcome all temptations moment by moment.
3. When we obey God and do what pleases Him, our hearts will not condemn us and we will have confidence in prayer.
4. Our prayers must include asking God to give us a tender conscience—even in the small things.

3. In answer to prayer, God may stretch us beyond human endurance and intelligence so our work will be truly His work within us and not ours alone.

4. We need to rejoice and think about how much God strongly desires to work with us.

29. *Our Work or God's Work*   245
    (*Job 1:21–22*)
    1. God promises that by His grace He will give us all that we need to honour Him in an unbelieving world.
    2. We need to learn that we will honour God the most when we allow His character to shine forth from our lives.
    3. We can become a friend of God and be used by God as His friend by walking in the Spirit.
    4. God may allow testing so we can show others that we truly believe that whatever we have achieved is really God's work or achievement, and not ours.

30. *Jesus' Prayer and God's Work in Us*   253
    (*John 17:14–18*)
    1. A life of prayerful obedience will lead us to confront an unbelieving world and

a rebellious church with the exclusive claims of Jesus Christ.
2.   The more we pray and obey, the more intense the spiritual battle can become.

31. *Life After Death*   261
     (*Psalm 32:6*)
     1.   By His Spirit, God often gives widows, or widowers, more opportunities to serve Him and demonstrates His power to overcome their tragic loss.
     2.   Love as the motive will keep our prayers from becoming legalistic.

Epilogue   269
     1.   If we measure our success and failures by the impact or size of great Christian leaders, we may always be disappointed.
     2.   No matter what role God wants us to take in His Kingdom, He will use enduring principles and similar procedures over and over again to teach people how to pray, to draw people close to Him, to transform their character into the image of Christ, to enable them to lead some to saving faith, and to empower them to bear fruit.

STUDY GUIDE ON PRAYER FOR INDIVIDUALS, CHURCH GROUPS, SUNDAY SCHOOLS AND HOMES

The five questions keyed to each chapter can be used for a personal review of your daily reading and to guide you in making a personal prayer journal of what you are learning about prayer and how God is answering your prayers. The questions are also designed to be freely discussed by groups. If the book is to be used by a continuing prayer group, you will probably only want to study one chapter at each meeting in order to have plenty of time for individual and group prayer, as well as discussion on the application of the principles you are learning. At the end of thirty-one weeks or the ten-week study, you might want to review and discuss what you believe are the most important points about prayer made in the book. You might also want to discuss any of the prayer principles that are listed in Appendix I: these by no means exhaust all of the principles in each meditation, but are provided for a brief summary of the chapter. After you complete your study, I would be interested in learning how the book has helped you or your group, and any suggestions you might have for changes or other books. Write to:

L. G. Parkhurst, Jr.,
PO Box 571,
Edmond,
Oklahoma,
73083-0571,
USA.

WEEK 1

Open with praise and thanksgiving to God, and pray for the Holy Spirit to open hearts and minds to receive God's truth and encouragement regarding prayer.

2. Before and after we give a Bible to a Jew, what specific things should we pray for God to do in their lives with the Bible?
3. If an unbeliever is not a Jew, what different specific things should we pray about before and after we give them the Bible?
4. When we keep on praying for some unbelievers year after year, what are some specific things the Holy Spirit may show us to add to our prayer requests?
5. What are some other dangers we and others may face as we witness that we need to make a matter of prayer?

3. *God Comforts in Many Ways*   37
    (2 Corinthians 1:3–4, 10–11)
    1. Are there any people you especially remember who encouraged you by their faith and prayers in their troubles?
    2. What might have happened if the Schaeffers had not taken the time to care for, pray for, and encourage others to pray for, the young pastor who knocked on their door?
    3. If God anticipates our needs and wants to meet them, why should we pray?
    4. Why would Paul write to the Corinthians and tell them how important

their prayers were for him, especially since he was an apostle?

5. Can you think of some answers to your prayers that might encourage others to learn more about prayer and pray more?

Write down some personal and group prayer requests with the date. When an answer is received, write down the date of God's answer. Be prepared to share, discuss and praise God for any answers.

WEEK 2

Open with praise and thanksgiving to God, and pray for the Holy Spirit to open hearts and minds to receive God's truth and encouragement regarding prayer. Share any answers to prayer, and thank God in prayer for these answers.

4. ***God Has Provided Before We Pray***   45
    (*Matthew 6:6–8*)

1. Why does God want us to pray about and do even 'small' things; such as spending time preparing for and conducting family prayers, Bible studies and worship?

2. What are some reasons for making our prayers very specific sometimes, but at other times more general?

3. In very specific prayers especially, why should we be careful to pray and insist before God that we want to be submissive to His will whatever it is?

4. Why does God want us to give Him reasons for our prayer requests?

5. Why should we think about 'being fair' to others when we pray for specific blessings for ourselves? For example, how could we wisely pray for a heart transplant if we needed one?

5. *Learning to Pray*   53
   (*Luke 11:1*)
   1. Can anyone live and pray in such a way
      that they will encourage others to pray,
      or is this only for special people?
   2. Why does someone first have to know
      Jesus Christ is their Lord and Saviour
      before they can pray effectively?
   3. What are some ways we can use the
      Bible more effectively to teach others
      about prayer?
   4. What are some things we can say and
      do to encourage new believers to pray
      and believe that God will answer their
      prayers?
   5. What are some of the benefits, as well as
      the dangers, of setting conditions as we
      pray in total submission to the will of
      God?

6. *Praying for New Things*   61
   (*Deuteronomy 4:7*)
   1. What are some situations that you have
      been in where you could only turn to
      God for help?
   2. Why do some people think that they
      should not bother God with small
      things?
   3. What are some things that 'living by

faith' has not protected you from, and
how can (or has) prayer helped?
4. Do you know of any situations in your
life where God has brought good out of
evil and blessed you or others in answer
to prayer?
5. What are some *false* promises that some
can make when trying to convince
others to live by faith?

Write down some personal and group prayer
requests with the date. When an answer is
received, write down the date of God's answer. Be
prepared to share, discuss and praise God for any
answers.

WEEK 3

Open with praise and thanksgiving to God, and pray for the Holy Spirit to open hearts and minds to receive God's truth and encouragement regarding prayer. Share any answers to prayer, and thank God in prayer for these answers.

7. *Living by Faith*   69
    (*Matthew 6:24–26*)
    1. What does 'living by faith' mean?
    2. What are some ways every Christian lives by faith as God teaches them how to pray?
    3. Why does God teach us about prayer step by step, rather than all at once?
    4. What effect can early training have in regard to learning how to pray, and what are some ways this training can be overcome if it has not been helpful?
    5. If some we know are troubled by unbelieving children, parents, husband or wife, what can we say that will encourage them to keep on living by faith and praying for them?

    lead others to salvation, rather than just one or the other?

2. Why can't we just give *everybody* the same three or four truths in a formula and be successful in evangelism with everyone we talk to?

3. What are some traits that people have when they witness with a wrong spirit or attitude, and what are the dangers of witnessing in the wrong spirit?

4. What does it mean to have an 'obligation' to pray for others, and what dangers can come from our failing to intercede for others?

5. Over the last three weeks, what are some of the things you have learned about the Holy Spirit and His work?

Write down some personal and group prayer requests with the date. When an answer is received, write down the date of God's answer. Be prepared to share, discuss and praise God for any answers.

WEEK 4

Open with praise and thanksgiving to God, and pray for the Holy Spirit to open hearts and minds to receive God's truth and encouragement regarding prayer. Share any answers to prayer, and thank God in prayer for these answers.

10. *When God Moves Slowly*   93
    (*2 Thessalonians 3:1*)

    1. Rather than just ignore those who express a disinterest in Christianity, what *specific* things can we do and what *specific* things can we ask God to do on their behalf?

    2. Why is it so important for us to let others see our good works in addition to our praying for them and teaching them the truth (see Matthew 5:13–16)?

    3. Should we seek the type of experience in prayer that God gave Edith regarding Dr Otten? If so, what are the dangers as well as the rewards of doing so?

    4. What are some good reasons for God delaying in answering our prayers, and how can we pray differently as God delays?

5.   Why do you think God led Fran to write
      his first book on the Bible, but delayed
      its publication for twenty years, until
      after he had written and published
      some other books?

11. *God Gives More than We Ask*   101
     (*Ephesians 3:20–21*)
     1.   What are the practical implications of
           God reigning as Lord over the whole of
           life, and how does this affect the scope
           of our prayers?
     2.   If Christ is Lord over the whole of life,
           should   we   distinguish   between
           'spiritual things' and other things as
           we pray? If so, why?
     3.   How can our knowing that God *always*
           has wise and loving reasons for all that
           He does affect what we pray for, who to
           pray for, and how to pray?
     4.   What difference would it make in our
           praise to God, if we always looked for
           the manifold blessings that follow from
           His answers to our prayers for only one
           need?
     5.   Can you see, and share with others,
           some of the ways God has been using to
           develop your thinking ability and

expand your circle of concern in your prayers?

   1. What difference will it make in our life of prayer when we realise that we have a satanic adversary?
   2. What are some of the reasons God allows Satan to attack us from time to time, and not just tempt us?
   3. Since we do not seek a hayloft to duplicate Fran's spiritual reawakening, what do we need to do to revive our spirits?
   4. What are some ways God can use material provisions or their lack to manifest His will to us through prayer?
   5. What reasons could you give a person *who did not believe in prayer* for God's delaying His answers to prayer sometimes?

Write down some personal and group prayer requests with the date. When an answer is received, write down the date of God's answer. Be prepared to share, discuss and praise God for any answers.

WEEK 5

Open with praise and thanksgiving to God, and pray for the Holy Spirit to open hearts and minds to receive God's truth and encouragement regarding prayer. Share any answers to prayer, and thank God in prayer for these answers.

13. **The Battle in Prayer and the Bible**   117
    (*Daniel 9:2–3*)

    1. Can you think of other situations when you could apply God's promise in Proverbs 21:1 when you pray?

    2. List some things we can pray about from both the Old and New Testament commands, as well as the Bible's promises and the examples of others in the Bible?

    3. Why do you think Daniel prayed, pleaded and fasted in deep humility for God to do what He had promised to do already?

    4. Are there some Bible verses, promises or predictions that you use often when you pray, such as Romans 8:28?

    5. Why is daily Bible reading in the context of prayer so important?

3. Today, what would a 'House of Prayer' be like?

4. Why do some people seem to withdraw from involvement in the world, as salt and light, the more they pray?

5. Why does God sometimes work so closely to the deadline when meeting our needs?

Write down some personal and group prayer requests with the date. When an answer is received, write down the date of God's answer. Be prepared to share, discuss and praise God for any answers.

WEEK 6

Open with praise and thanksgiving to God, and pray for the Holy Spirit to open hearts and minds to receive God's truth and encouragement regarding prayer. Share any answers to prayer, and thank God in prayer for these answers.

16. *My Father's Plans*   141
    (Jeremiah 29:11–13)
    1. How would you define or describe true faith?
    2. Does the definition of true faith in the chapter include too much or too little?
    3. What are some reasons for insisting that our faith and prayer requests rest on good and sufficient evidence?
    4. What are the means God uses to lead us to pray according to His will?
    5. What are some reasons God will not often show us His plans all at once?

17. *My Father's Provisions*   149
    (Isaiah 56:6–7)
    1. What are some things you could do to make your own home or church a house of prayer?
    2. Why does the Bible put so much

emphasis on loving God in addition to serving and worshipping God? Why isn't serving God sufficient?

3.   What four aspects of their work did the Schaeffers commit to prayer, and is there a way for churches or others to commit themselves to similar vows without trying to duplicate or copy L'Abri?

4.   What does it mean to make a vow to God, and what are the implications of this in the spiritual battle?

5.   How is real choice involved in prayer and making vows?

18. *My Father's People*   157
     (*Isaiah 45:20*)

1.   How was God's honour involved in the Schaeffers' prayers for money to buy their home and stay in Switzerland?

2.   What would you say to someone who says we should only pray for spiritual blessings and never for material things?

3.   Why do you think God would prefer to involve a large number of people giving small gifts to start L'Abri instead of a few people giving large gifts, and why has this been a pattern most of the time through the years?

4. Why do you think God leads us to the point of desperation sometimes when we are praying for Him to take care of us?
5. What are some of the ways in which living by faith and prayer can involve more work than we have ever done before?

Write down some personal and group prayer requests with the date. When an answer is received, write down the date of God's answer. Be prepared to share, discuss and praise God for any answers.

WEEK 7

Open with praise and thanksgiving to God, and pray for the Holy Spirit to open hearts and minds to receive God's truth and encouragement regarding prayer. Share any answers to prayer, and thank God in prayer for these answers.

19. *Living Before Others*   165
     (1 Timothy 2:8)

1.   Name some reasons and explain why we must allow God to develop our Christian character and lead us to moral and spiritual maturity.

2.   What does it mean to bow metaphysically and morally?

3.   What are some of the things that will supernaturally flow forth from our lives after we accept the finished work of Christ personally?

4.   Why should we pray for the Holy Spirit to empower us to live exemplary Christian lives?

5.   Why and how does God use *both* the Truth of His Word and the Holy Spirit to sanctify us or help us live with true spirituality?

309

3. What are some reasons God wants to bless united prayer and answer the requests of prayer groups?
4. Why shouldn't we force everyone to fast when a day of fasting is called for, and why should we be considerate of those who cannot or do not want to fast?
5. What are some reasons for fasting in a time of crisis?

Write down some personal and group prayer requests with the date. When an answer is received, write down the date of God's answer. Be prepared to share, discuss and praise God for any answers.

WEEK 8

Open with praise and thanksgiving to God, and pray for the Holy Spirit to open hearts and minds to receive God's truth and encouragement regarding prayer. Share any answers to prayer, and thank God in prayer for these answers.

22. *Confidence in Prayer and our Conscience* 189
    (1 John 3:21–22)
    1. Why is it so important for Christians to remember that they are adopted sons and daughters of their Heavenly Father and not just servants of the Most High God?
    2. When praying to God, how can we be sure that we love the Giver more than the gifts He gives, and what are some of the indications that this is true for us?
    3. Why is confession and repentance of sin so important when coming to God in prayer?
    4. How can we have a clean conscience and keep it clean?
    5. Why do some say that almost any concern to be holy is being legalistic, and how can we respond to them?

   1.   Do you agree or disagree with the following statement, and why or why not: 'Only the prayers of righteous people are powerful and effective'?

   2.   What does it mean to be righteous in Christ, and how can we be?

   3.   How would you define or describe a 'new creature in Christ', and how should that make a difference in our life of prayer from those who do not know Christ?

   4.   What are some things we must do to demonstrate the righteous acts of Jesus Christ to both believers and unbelievers?

   5.   Why must the Holy Spirit play such a prominent role in our righteousness and in teaching us how to pray effectively?

   1.   What are some of the *wrong* ideas we need to avoid with regard to prayer and why God answers prayer?

   2.   When we spend time in self-evaluation, how can we avoid becoming too

            introspective and harming our prayer
            life?

3.   What are some of the real benefits from
            God delaying to answer our prayers as
            quickly as we expect?

4.   What are some possible reasons for our
            prayers not being answered quickly?

5.   What are some reasons for keeping on
            and praising and glorifying God when
            He seems to be delaying His answer to
            our prayers day after day?

Write down some personal and group prayer
requests with the date. When an answer is
received, write down the date of God's answer. Be
prepared to share, discuss and praise God for any
answers.

WEEK 9

Open with praise and thanksgiving to God, and pray for the Holy Spirit to open hearts and minds to receive God's truth and encouragement regarding prayer. Share any answers to prayer, and thank God in prayer for these answers.

25. ***Prayer and Hard Work***   213
    (Matthew 9:36–38)
    1. Why must we be so careful not to manipulate people by the way we pray, even if we think our intentions are worthy?
    2. What are some things that can be gained from praying only for those of the Lord's choice to come to us for help, to join our church, to work in ministry with us?
    3. Why will some of God's answers to our prayers lead to our working harder than we have ever worked before?
    4. Why will living by faith and prayer teach us to appreciate the little things and the little people, as much as the big things and great people?
    5. What would life be like if prayer could replace hard work?

26. *Prayer and Sacrifice*   221
(*Colossians 1:10; 4:3–4*)

1. Did those who followed Jesus in New Testament times live for themselves supremely or for Him?

2. Can our willingness to sacrifice for God and His work be an indication of whether or not we truly accept Jesus as our Saviour and Lord?

3. How can we avoid the trap of trying to obligate God to us so that He will hear our prayers as we try to fulfil the conditions He has set forth to answer our prayers?

4. What can happen if we try to get others to sacrifice to promote our work, rather than pray for God to move us and others to make any needed sacrifices to promote His work?

5. Why must we continually remind people that God will not require us to 'make bricks without straw', as Pharaoh required of the Jews in Egypt, but will provide us with all we need and more to do His work in His way in answer to prayer?

27. *Prayer and Growth*   229
    (*Acts 2:42*)

1.   Describe some of the differences between the world's and God's ideas of success and how this can relate to what things people pray for God to give them.

2.   What problems can we anticipate and pray about if God grants us His idea of success?

3.   What do we mean by prayer becoming 'a state of mind', and how do we attain that state?

4.   What are some indicators that we are being faithful as we pray and work?

5.   What can the difference be between devotion in our prayers and doing our devotions, and how would you teach a new believer the difference?

Write down some personal and group prayer requests with the date. When an answer is received, write down the date of God's answer. Be prepared to share, discuss and praise God for any answers.

WEEK 10

Open with praise and thanksgiving to God, and pray for the Holy Spirit to open hearts and minds to receive God's truth and encouragement regarding prayer. Share any answers to prayer, and thank God in prayer for these answers.

28. *Asking Great Things from God*   237
    (*1 Chronicles 17:25*)
    1. How can we use the promises of God in His Word to give us the courage to pray for great things, without falling into the temptation of praying from the worldly view of success?
    2. What must we do in our prayer life to keep from pride if God blesses us with great answers to prayer and does great things publicly through us?
    3. Why must we always pray from a loving intention whenever we ask great things from God?
    4. How can we determine what is worthy of our labours if so many more requests than we can possibly meet come to us in answer to prayer?
    5. How can we maintain the attitude of wanting to be used by God rather than

falling into the temptation of wanting to use God through prayer?

29. *Our Work or God's Work*   245
(Job 1:21–22)
   1.   What must we do to be worthy to ask great things from God?
   2.   What are some indications that we are a friend of God, and how will this understanding affect the way we approach God in prayer from other ways?
   3.   What does this mean to you: 'We will honour God the most when we allow His character to shine forth from our lives,' and what do we need to pray for in order to do this in the troubled and evil world in which we live?
   4.   What must we guard against, and what will our prayers need to include, if God gives us a 'celebrity ministry'?
   5.   How can God's testing of our ministry or work influence the way we pray, especially if we discover that our success in work or ministry has led us to change our motives for what we do?

whatever we want through prayer, if we just have enough faith?

2. Why can facing death be so difficult, and what can we say to others and pray to God as they face death or the death of a loved one?

3. How can we use Edith Schaeffer's prayer life as an example to encourage single people and senior citizens to pray and seek God's leading in their lives and not give up?

4. What are some things we can pray and do so each person will be special to us and feel special when we talk with them?

5. What should I do next, now that I have completed this study of prayer?

Write down some personal and group prayer requests with the date. When an answer is received, write down the date of God's answer. Be prepared to share, discuss and praise God for any answers.

APPENDIX III

WHERE TO FIND L'ABRI

BRITISH L'*Abri*
The Manor House,
Greatham,
Hampshire,
United Kingdom,
GU33 6HF
[Telephone: Blackmoor 436]
(Audio tape catalogues available upon request)

DUTCH L'Abri
Kromme Niewe Gracht 90,
3512 HM Utrecht,
Holland
[Telephone: (030) 31 69133]

SWEDISH L'Abri
Per Staffan and Lisa Johansson,
Ryggasstugan,
Ransvik,
N. Strandvagen 72,
260 42 Molle,
Sweden

SWISS L'Abri
Chalet Bellevue,
1861 Huemoz,
Switzerland
[Telephone: (025) 35 21 39]

USA L'Abri
L'Abri Fellowship Foundation,
1465 12th Avenue N.E.,
Rochester,
Minnesota 55906
[Telephone: (507) 282 3292]

L'Abri Fellowship,
49 Lynbrook Road,
Southborough,
Massachusetts 01772
[Telephone: (617) 481 6490]

You may also learn more about Francis and Edith Schaeffer, and their continuing influence, by writing to:

The Francis A. Schaeffer Foundation,
100 Hardscrabble Road,
Braircliff Manor,
New York 10510
[Telephone: (914) 747 9102]

ENDNOTES

Edith Schaeffer's Thoughts on Prayer

1. Edith Schaeffer, *With Love, Edith* (San Francisco: Harper & Row, 1988), 137. Letter from Switzerland, February 28, 1950.

2. Edith Schaeffer, *Dear Family* (San Francisco: Harper & Row, 1989), 21. Letter from Switzerland, July 21, 1961.

3. Edith Schaeffer, *The Tapestry: The Life and Times of Francis and Edith Schaeffer* (Waco: Word Books, 1981, Special Memorial Edition 1984), 58, 126. The Schaeffers' autobiography.

Preface

1. Edith Schaeffer, *L'Abri* (Wheaton: Tyndale House Publishers, 1969), 124, 125.

2. See Francis A. Schaeffer, *He is There and He is Not Silent* in *The Complete Works of Francis A. Schaeffer: A Christian Worldview*, 'A Christian View of Philosophy and Culture' (Westchester: Crossway Books, 1982), Volume One, 273–352.

3. My previous book on Dr Francis Schaeffer was a brief biography that tried to explain or interpret his apologetics for lay people: see *Francis Schaeffer: The Man and His Message* (Wheaton: Tyndale

House Publishers, 1985 and Eastbourne: Kingsway Publications, 1986). When I compiled and edited Edith Schaeffer's *The Art of Life* (Wheaton: Crossway Books, 1987 and Eastbourne: Kingsway Publications, 1988), I put some of Edith's basic teachings on creativity and life in a devotional book, but omitted any discussions on prayer. Most recently, Edith Schaeffer has published *The Life of Prayer* (Wheaton: Crossway Books, 1992), but this book does not discuss their personal answers to prayer in light of their own prayer principles and the Scriptures. Nor does the book use a devotional format of daily readings. I hope that after you read *How God Teaches Us to Pray*, you will be inspired to read Edith's book *The Life of Prayer*.

4. Some of Dr Schaeffer's sermons on prayer are available on tapes from *L'Abri*. These are *Framework for Prayer* 26.3 and *Prayer Series* 24.2, 24.3, 26.1, 26.2. A listing of most of Dr Schaeffer's tapes are in the American edition of *Francis Schaeffer: The Man and His Message*, 229–241, but for reasons unknown to the author this was excluded from the British edition.

5. Francis Schaeffer, *Letters of Francis A. Schaeffer*, edited with introductions by Lane T. Dennis (Westchester, Crossway Books, 1985).

6. Edith Schaeffer's family letters were published in her *With Love, Edith* , 458 pages, and in her *Dear Family*, 428 pages. The story of their lives is found in *L'Abri* and in her autobiography, *The Tapestry*, 654 pages. Her two books of letters and

The Tapestry are now out of print. All quotations from the Schaeffers' books are from these three out of print books. References to their books still in print will be found in these Endnotes.

7. Edith Schaeffer was born in China to parents who were missionaries in the China Inland Mission. She learned many of her ideas about prayer from the godly examples of these missionaries. L'Abri inherited much from Hudson Taylor's teachings and his life of prayer. Prayer meetings were established in England and all over the world for Hudson Taylor's work, just as people from all over the world have interceded for the Schaeffer's and L'Abri as the L'Abri Praying Family. See also the books I have compiled and edited from the writings of Charles G. Finney: Charles G. Finney, *Answers to Prayer* (Minneapolis: Bethany House Publishers, 1983); *Principles of Prayer* (Minneapolis: Bethany House Publishers, 1980); *Principles of Devotion* (Minneapolis: Bethany House Publishers, 1987). Nelson Word Ltd. has also published my Andrew Murray and C. H. Spurgeon, *The Believer's Secret of Intercession* (Milton Keynes: Word Publishing, 1989) and Andrew Murray and Brother Lawrence, *The Believer's Secret of the Abiding Presence* (Milton Keynes: Word Publishing, 1989).

8. A. W. Tozer, *Let My People Go: The Life of Robert A. Jaffray* (Camp Hill: Christian Publications, 1990), 1.

9. See also, L. G. Parkhurst, Jr., 'The Quiet Assurance of Truth' in *Francis A. Schaeffer*:

Portraits of the Man and His Work, edited by Lane T. Dennis, (Westchester: Crossway Books, 1986), 141–151.

10. It would have been impossible for me to try and capture Edith's style of writing in this book, and I have not tried. Each writer's style, just as each Christian's prayer life, will be intensely personal. I do encourage you to read Edith's books for yourself, and I hope this book will inspire you to do so.

11. He often said that *True Spirituality* was the most important book he ever wrote and the only one he ever reread to keep in touch with the reality of what he was doing. Francis A. Schaeffer, *True Spirituality* in *The Complete Works of Francis A. Schaeffer: A Christian Worldview*, 'A Christian View of Spirituality', Volume Three, 195–378. See also the important books, *The Church Before the Watching World* and *The Mark of the Christian* in *The Complete Works*, 'A Christian View of the Church', Volume Four, 113–205.

12. Dr Schaeffer died of cancer in Rochester, Minnesota, in 1984. Mrs Schaeffer still makes her home there, and works with the L'Abri branch they founded in Rochester.

1. If the Answer is No

1. Edith Schaeffer, *Dear Family*, 22. See also Edith Schaeffer, 'If God is Sovereign, Why Pray?' in *The Life of Prayer*, 205–221.

2. *Praying for Unbelievers*

1. Edith Schaeffer, *Christianity is Jewish* (Wheaton: Tyndale House Publishers, 1975); Edith Schaeffer, *Forever Music* (Grand Rapids: Baker Book House, 1986 and 1992); Franz Mohr with Edith Schaeffer, *My Life with the Great Pianists* (Grand Rapids: Baker Book House, 1992). The book by Mohr (with Edith Schaeffer) will especially encourage Christians who have secular jobs. It shows how Mohr prayed for people, sometimes for years, for God to prepare their hearts and give him the opportunity to tell them about Jesus when they had a receptive mind.

2. You can learn how to buy Prophecy Editions of the New Testament by writing to Million Testaments Campaigns, 1211 Arch Street, Philadelphia, Pennsylvania 19107, USA.

3. Francis A. Schaeffer and C. Everett Koop MD, *Whatever Happened to the Human Race?* (Old Tappan: Fleming H. Revell, 1979 and Wheaton: Crossway Books, 1985); Edith Schaeffer, *Affliction* (Old Tappan: Fleming H. Revell Company, 1978); Francis A. Schaeffer, *The God Who is There* (Downers Grove: Intervarsity Press, 1968). Before his death in 1984, Dr Schaeffer edited and combined his works in the five-volume set: *The Complete Works of Francis A. Schaeffer*. The newest edition of *Affliction* is scheduled to be published by Baker Book House of Grand Rapids, Michigan in 1993.

4. Edith Schaeffer, *L'Abri: New Expanded Edition*

(Wheaton: Crossway Books, 1992). First edition published in 1969.

4. *God Has Provided Before We Pray*

1. Edith Schaeffer, *With Love, Edith*, 99.

5. *Learning To Pray*

1. Edith Schaeffer, *With Love, Edith*, 110.

2. For her specific teachings on prayer, see Edith Schaeffer, *The Life of Prayer*.

7. *Living by Faith*

1. See Dr and Mrs Howard Taylor, *J. Hudson Taylor: God's Man in China* (Chicago: Moody Press, 1965).

8. *Passing On Our Faith*

1. See George Müller, *The Autobiography of George Müller*, edited by H. Lincoln Wayland, (Grand Rapids: Baker Book House, 1981, reprinted from the 1861 edition).

2. Edith Schaeffer, *With Love, Edith*, 237.

3. Edith Schaeffer, *With Love, Edith*, 251.

4. *Daily Light* is a collection of various Bible verses selected for a brief daily reading and available in many different translations, languages and editions.

10. *When God Moves Slowly*

1. Edith Schaeffer, *With Love, Edith*, 273.

2. These lessons were eventually published by Francis Schaeffer as *Basic Bible Studies* (Wheaton: Tyndale House Publishers, 1972). Some people have become Christians in my churches as the direct result of group studies of this book.

12. *The Battle in Prayer and Satan*

1. Edith Schaeffer, *With Love, Edith*, 275.

2. Edith Schaeffer's book *Affliction* is probably the best book on the question of affliction and the spiritual battle we face as Christians. First published by Revell in 1978, a new edition is scheduled by Baker Book House in 1993.

3. These lectures were later revised and published as *True Spirituality* (Wheaton: Tyndale House Publishers, 1971 and in *The Complete Works*, Volume Three). Fran believed that God gave these lectures to him as the foundation of all that was to follow in his life and for the beginning of L'Abri.

14. *Praying Through the Promises of God*

1. To learn the exciting story of the founding of L'Abri, the many answers to prayer and the Lord's protection they received, read Edith Schaeffer, *L'Abri: New Expanded Edition*.

15. *My Father's House*

1. Edith Schaeffer, *With Love, Edith*, 288.

2. Edith Schaeffer, *With Love, Edith*, 319.

3. In *The Tapestry*, Edith called this answering prayer 'backwards', 421.

4. Edith Schaeffer, *With Love, Edith*, 324.

17. *My Father's Provisions*

1. Edith Schaeffer, *The Tapestry*, 420.

19. *Living Before Others*

1. See especially Francis A. Schaeffer, *True Spirituality* (Volume Three, 195–378); *The Church Before the Watching World* and *The Mark of the Christian* (Volume Four, 113–205) in *The Complete Works of Francis A. Schaeffer: A Christian Worldview*; also *The Great Evangelical Disaster* (Wheaton: Crossway Books, 1984).

2. In many ways, accomplishing this feat daily for more than thirty years shows the wonder-working power of God more than many other answers to prayer in the Schaeffers' and similar books. For a similar example from the nineteenth century, you can read about the answers to prayer of America's greatest revivalist in Charles G. Finney, *Answers to Prayer*. When one studies the Schaeffers' work in depth, one discovers that their work in L'Abri was one of almost continuous revival for more than thirty years. This chapter and those that follow teach some of the secrets of maintaining a personal work of revival: the practice of biblical Christianity in the power of the Holy Spirit.

22. *Confidence in Prayer and Our Conscience*

1. Also, Andrew Murray and Brother Lawrence, *The Believer's Secret of the Abiding Presence*. Brother Lawrence practised the presence of Christ much like the Schaeffers; however, the Schaeffers did so while constantly surrounded by unbelievers.

23. *Prayer and Righteousness*

1. See especially Dr Schaeffer's last book, *The Great Evangelical Disaster*.

25. *Prayer and Hard Work*

1. Edith Schaeffer, *Dear Family*, 103.

2. Edith Schaeffer, *With Love, Edith*, 438.

3. Edith Schaeffer, *Dear Family*, 94.

26. *Prayer and Sacrifice*

1. Edith Schaeffer, *Dear Family*, 26.

28. *Asking Great Things from God*

1. Francis Schaeffer, *How Should We Then Live?* (Wheaton: Crossway Books, 1983: first published in 1976). Francis Schaeffer and C. Everett Koop, MD, *Whatever Happened to the Human Race?* Films by Gospel Films.

2. Francis Schaeffer, *A Christian Manifesto,* (Wheaton: Crossway Books, 1981) and *The Great Evangelical Disaster.*

3. Eventually, Francis Schaeffer's picture would be featured prominently on the book covers of *Great Leaders of the Christian Church,* edited by John D. Woodbridge, (Chicago: Moody Press, 1988); Christopher Catherwood, *Five Evangelical Leaders,* (Wheaton: Harold Shaw Publishers, 1985), and L. G. Parkhurst, Jr., *Francis Schaeffer: The Man and His Message.*

4. They named Farel House after a Swiss Reformer who preceded Calvin, because he was one of the warmest and most understanding of the Reformers. His spirit and temper was one that those in L'Abri wanted to model. Many of Fran's taped lectures were first made for Farel House students.

31. *Life After Death*

1. See especially: Edith Schaeffer, *Forever Music*, and Edith Schaeffer, *The Art of Life*.

2. For a good description of this type of prayer life and how to practise it, see Andrew Murray and Brother Lawrence, *The Believer's Secret of the Abiding Presence*.

3. See Edith Schaeffer, *The Life of Prayer*.

INDEX TO THE SCRIPTURES

How God Teaches Us to Pray

ABOUT THE AUTHOR

L. G. Parkhurst has known the Schaeffers since 1978, and is the author of *Francis Schaeffer: The Man and His Message*. He is also the compiler and editor of Edith Schaeffer's devotional book, *The Art of Life*. He has compiled and edited numerous prayer books, including the following books published by Nelson Word Ltd.: *The Believer's Secret of the Abiding Presence* (from the writings of Andrew Murray and Brother Lawrence), *The Believer's Secret of Intercession* (from the writings of Andrew Murray and C. H. Spurgeon), and *How to Pray in the Spirit* (from the writings of John Bunyan). His other devotional book regarding why and how God has answered prayer, *Answers to Prayer*, is from the writings of America's foremost revivalist, Charles G. Finney, and shows how God promotes revival by the work of His Spirit.

L. G. Parkhurst has a Master of Divinity Degree from Princeton Theological Seminary and a Master of Arts Degree in Philosophy from the University of Oklahoma. He has been a pastor for more than twenty years, and has published more than 26 books, most of them on prayer and revival. He currently serves as the pastor of Bethel Congregational Church in Edmond, Oklahoma.

HOW TO PRAY IN THE SPIRIT

John Bunyan

Edited by L.G. Parkhurst, Jr.,

'True prayer is a sincere, sensible, affectionate pouring out of your heart and soul to God through Jesus Christ, in the strength and assistance of the Holy Spirit . . .'

John Bunyan lived at a time when, 'Those who pray with the Spirit, though ever so humble and holy, are counted as fanatics. Those who pray with the form of a written prayer only, and without the Spirit, are counted as virtuous.' In prison in 1662 for preaching in public, he learned that the only way to glorify God in his sufferings was to pray often and deeply, and his thoughts on prayer were forged on the anvil of religious persecution.

L.G. Parkhurst, Jr., has edited Bunyan's writings on prayer—simple, direct and rich in Scripture and its application—into daily meditations for today's English reader, adding his own prayer for each day. As Bunyan encourages us to pray in both spirit and mind, condemning the mechanicalness and hypocrisy that can attend the use of many prayer books and techniques, *How to Pray in the Spirit* will give you deeper insight and greater freedom of expression in your personal relationship with God through Christ.

Catalogue Number YB 9513   £3.99

PRAYER: KEY TO REVIVAL

Paul Y. Cho

The author shares the secret behind the phenomenal growth of the world's largest church—the Yoido Full Gospel Church of Seoul, Korea. Dr Cho points out, 'It is because I believe in revival and renewal that I have written this book. It has been historically true that prayer has been the key to every revival in the history of Christianity.'

Out of his personal experience as a pastor, Dr Cho answers such general questions as *why* to pray and *when* to pray. He also deals with such specific questions as:

- Why does fasting increase the effectiveness of prayer?
- What does prayer accomplish?
- What part does the Holy Spirit play in prayer?

'No man can schedule a revival,' Dr Cho has said, 'for God alone is the giver of life. But . . . when the "fullness of time" has come and prayer ascends from a few earnest hearts, then history teaches it is time for the tide of revival to sweep once more.'

Dr Cho bases his study on one simple premise: 'God has no favourite children. What has worked for me will also work for you . . . If God has worked through men and women in the past, *He can work through you.*'

'This is the best book I have ever read on prayer.'
Evangelism Today

Catalogue Number YB 9059   £1.95

GETTING THROUGH TO GOD

MICHAEL BAUGHEN

'*This wise, warm-hearted, down-to-earth book . . . could greatly enrich our praying and thereby get us growing again. I hope it will. It did me good to read it ; I hope it will do good to many more.*'

James I. Packer

In this basic book on prayer, Michael Baughen considers the foundations of faith in God, the character of God, the purposes of God and the ways of God, and helps the readers to a perspective which avoids the problems created by a wrong understanding and approach to prayer.

He is intensely practical. When should we pray? For what, or whom? Should we pray that sick people should be healed, or simply leave it to God? And he deals simply and straightforwardly with the most common problems in prayer—'unanswered' prayer, unbelief, superstition and so on.

There are few individuals who will not find their whole approach to prayer sharpened by this book, and few churches that would not find their spiritual temperature raised if it were the subject of group study.

Michael Baughen says, 'This little book . . . is useless unless it affects the prayer-life of its readers. I hope it will yours, perhaps by radical overhaul, or by practical action or by taking up some new emphasis . . . All prayer starts and ends with God, so "Rejoice in the Lord always." '

Catalogue Number YB 9566   Full colour, hardback £7.99

HOW TO LISTEN TO GOD

CHARLES STANLEY

'Nothing is more urgent, nothing more necessary, nothing more rewarding than hearing what God has to say. His voice waits to be heard and, having heard it, we are launched into the greatest, most exciting adventure we could ever imagine.'

Charles Stanley

Amidst the noise and constant activity in life, God's voice, once so important, has become but one voice among the many others that claim our attention. Yet it is the only voice that gives us access to the purity of a relationship with God Himself.

This book clearly helps the reader to discover and rediscover the voice of God. Charles Stanley presents examples of personal lessons he has learnt in how to listen to and be obedient to God, so that He can prove that He is both able and eager to communicate with us on a personal basis.

In order to enjoy the life God has given to us, we need to learn to listen to God's voice and experience His presence. The author's practical tips and guidelines will enable us to benefit from the fruits and gifts of His Spirit to the full in our lives.

Catalogue Number YB 9548   £3.99